Generational Trauma: An Overview

Generational Trauma: An Overview

Written by: John Christy Johnston, Peter Anto Johnson, Alyssa Wu, Rushmi Jamil, Yash Joshi, & Nazihah Alam

Edited by: Austin Mardon, Kathryn Carson, Sheher-Bano Ahmed

Designed by: Josh Kramer

Published by Golden Meteorite Press
2021

Generational Trauma: An Overview
Copyright © 2021 by Austin Mardon
All rights reserved.

This book or any portion thereof may not be reproduced or used in any manner whatsoever without the express written permission of the publisher except for the use of brief quotations in a review.

First Printing: 2021

ISBN: 978-1-77369-626-3

Golden Meteorite Press
103 11919 82 St NW
Edmonton, AB T5B 2W3
www.goldenmeteoritepress.com
aamardon@yahoo.ca
Alberta, Canada

Table of Contents

Chapter 1: What is Generational Trauma?   1
Chapter 2: What is the Study of Epigenetics?   11
Chapter 3: How did we come to understand the link between epigenetics and generational trauma?   21
Chapter 4: How do we study Epigenetics?   31
Chapter 5: How do we study Generational Trauma?   41
Chapter 5: What are Epigenetic Factors?   53
Chapter 7: What questions does the discovery of the link between events of history and generational trauma create?   65
Chapter 8: Why is it important to study Epigenetics?   75
Chapter 9: Does Generational Trauma Really Exist?   83
Chapter 10: How are epigenetic theories used in practice?   93
References   105

Chapter 1: What is Generational Trauma?

John Christy Johnston

Introduction

Generational trauma is a complex term that describes the phenomenon whereby trauma is transferred from generation to generation through biological as well as psychological means. Generational trauma may also be referred to as transgenerational trauma or intergenerational trauma. This notion of generational trauma has been linked as a manifestation of post-traumatic stress disorder or PTSD, which has been well-documented. Generational trauma is often described as a form of complex PTSD or cPTSD, a response to repetitive, frequent exposures to interpersonal trauma. Additionally, we will also consider some famous examples of generational trauma as an introduction to subsequent discussions of this topic. This chapter will attempt to examine the complexities of generational trauma.

DSM-5 Definition

The Diagnostic and Statistical Manual of Mental Disorders, 5th Edition (DSM-5) is the authoritative manual in clinical psychology and other aspects of mental health synthesized over a decade of work by international experts. The 5th edition represents the most up-to-date version, and has undergone significant changes and revisions from previous editions.

In the fourth edition of the DSM, trauma, or more specifically PTSD, was cast under the cluster of anxiety disorders. DSM-5 took it a step further and revised the disorder class for PTSD from 'Anxiety Disorders' to 'Trauma- and Stressor-Related Disorders,' widely regarded to be a more accurate assessment. (1) An independent study undertaken by the Substance Abuse and Mental Health Services Administration sought to understand these definitions of trauma in the context of children. Below is a short adapted summary of the six major DSM-5 criteria for PTSD:

> A. Exposure to actual or threatened death, serious injury, or sexual violence in one or more of the following ways:
> - Directly experiencing the traumatic event(s).
> - Witnessing, in person, the event(s) as it occurred to others, especially primary caregivers.
> - Learning that the traumatic event(s) occurred to a parent or care-giving figure.
> Note: Witnessing does not include events that are witnessed only in electronic media, television, movies, or pictures.

B. Presence of one or more of the following symptoms associated with the traumatic event(s), beginning after the traumatic event(s) occurred:
- Recurrent, involuntary, and intrusive distressing memories of the traumatic event(s). Note: Spontaneous and intrusive memories may not necessarily appear distressing and may be expressed as play reenactment.
- Recurrent distressing dreams in which the content and/or effect of the dream are related to the traumatic event(s).
- Dissociative reactions (e.g., flashbacks) in which the child feels or acts as if the traumatic event(s) were recurring. (Such reactions may occur on a continuum, with the most extreme expression being a complete loss of awareness of present surroundings.) Such trauma reenactment may occur in play.
- Intense or prolonged psychological distress at exposure to internal or external cues that symbolize or resemble an aspect of the traumatic event(s).
- Marked psychological reactions to reminders of the traumatic event(s).

C. One or more of the following symptoms, representing either persistent avoidance of stimuli associated with the traumatic event(s), or negative alterations in cognitions and mood associated with the traumatic event, must be present, beginning after the traumatic event(s) or worsening after the event:
- Persistent avoidance of stimuli
- Avoidance of or efforts to avoid places or physical reminders that arouse recollections of the traumatic event(s).

- Avoidance of or efforts to avoid people, conversations, or interpersonal situations that arouse recollections of the traumatic event(s).
- Negative alterations in cognitions
- Substantially increased frequency of negative emotional states (e.g., fear, guilt, sadness, shame, confusion).
- Markedly diminished interest or participation in significant activities
- Socially withdrawn behavior
- Persistent reduction in expression of positive emotions.

D. Alterations in arousal and reactivity associated with the traumatic event(s), beginning or worsening after the traumatic event(s) occurred, as evidence by two (or more) of the following:
- Irritable behavior and angry outbursts (with little or no provocation) typically expressed as verbal or physical aggression toward people or objects (including extreme temper tantrums).
- Hyper-vigilance.
- Exaggerated startle response.
- Problems with concentration.
- Sleep disturbance (e.g., difficulty falling or staying asleep or restless sleep).

E. Duration of the disturbance is more than 1 month.

F. The disturbance causes clinically significant distress or impairment in relationships with parents, siblings, peers, or other caregivers or with school behavior.

While these criteria are good descriptions of PTSD and trauma, they do not adequately or explicitly address generational trauma that may or may not be a result of caregivers. That being said, critics of generational trauma suggest that the concept of biologically inherited trauma is non-existent and that studies that show such instances of generational trauma are flawed in their methodologies and semantics. However, it should be noted that there are social behavioural explanations to support the notion of generational trauma, which is much more commonly regarded as an evidence-based explanation of this most peculiar phenomena. (2)

C-PTSD

Complex PTSD or C-PTSD differs from PTSD as it is typically associated with repeated trauma as opposed to a single traumatic event. Both PTSD and C-PTSD can cause flashbacks, nightmares, insomnia, and induce feelings of intense fear and paranoia even though the danger has passed. C-PTSD is often referenced when considering the idea of the propagation of trauma to the next generation. However, the deep-rooted psychological and developmental impacts of C-PTSD earlier in life are often more severe than a single traumatic experience—so much so, in fact, that many experts believe that DSM-5 PTSD diagnostic criteria does not adequately describe the wide-ranging, long-lasting repercussions of C-PTSD. In this regard, early childhood trauma can be one way by which intergenerational trauma can be reproduced and promulgated. Additional to the symptoms of PTSD, cPTSD also includes (2):
- Difficulty controlling emotions. It's common for someone suffering from C-PTSD to lose control over their emotions, which can manifest as explosive anger, persistent sadness,

depression, and suicidal thoughts.
- Negative self-view. C-PTSD can cause a person to view themselves in a negative light. They may feel helpless, guilty, or ashamed. They often have a sense of being completely different from other people.
- Difficulty with relationships. Relationships may suffer due to difficulties trusting others and a negative self-view. A person with C-PTSD may avoid relationships or develop unhealthy relationships because that is what they knew in the past.
- Detachment from the trauma. A person may disconnect from themselves (depersonalization) and the world around them (derealisation). Some people might even forget their trauma.
- Loss of a system of meanings. This can include losing one's core beliefs, values, religious faith, or hope in the world and other people.

Famous examples of generational trauma

Famous examples of generational trauma include legacies of Western colonialism, cataclysmic events such as the Rwandan genocide, and the multigenerational impacts of the slavery of African-Americans. The transmission vehicle for generational trauma has been a topic of particular interest for historians, psychologists, and sociologists investigating these largely collective forms of trauma, that affect individuals one or two generations removed from major traumatic events, such as the atrocities in indigineous residential schools or the concentration camps in World War II. To this end, there are specific groups of people that exhibit more signs of general trauma, a few of which we will discuss in the next sections.

Generational trauma in Indigenous people of Canada

The systematic indoctrination of First Nations, Metis, and Inuit peoples in Canada, the implementation of residential schools, and displacement of indigenous folks from their native territories to cramped reserves all contributed to the considerably shorter life expectancies of First Nations, Métis, and Inuit persons in Canada. (3) Outcomes like this also indicate that this demographic bears the brunt of the systemic inequities in Canada, and as such, are likely to be disproportionately impacted by disaster and difficulty such as the spread of the COVID-19 pandemic, climate change, or the lack of water sanitation in reserves. Perhaps, this represents one modality by which Indigenous people continue to experience and in some sense, re-experience the trauma of being separated from loved ones, early deaths, and a marginalization from the mainstream. These outcomes are abysmal for a developed nation - especially one that boasts universal healthcare and high standards of living.

In a 2014 review, Bombay et al., (4) examined several studies looking at the intergenerational effects of Canadian residential schools, institutionalized by the Canadian government from the 1880s until the mid-1990s to facilitate the systemic indoctrination of Indigenous children and thereby, resolve the "Indian problem" as recorded in the original government texts. The schools would provide a substandard education that not only shamed children about their native culture, but also served to inundate them with mainstream European cultural norms, language, and attitudes. In recent months, the discovery of the remains of 215 students at the Kamloops Indian Residential School in the Province of British Columbia have sparked nationwide horror and heartbreak. (5) The consequences of historical atrocities continue to cause grief and trauma amongst Canadians, especially the First Nations community.

Dr. Bombay and colleagues surveyed children of survivors of these residential schools and demonstrated that these individuals struggled with psychological distress, suicidality, and learning difficulties. In some cases, this even extended to grandchildren of survivors. Furthermore, the generations of Indigenous peoples who had undergone the residential schools were also more likely to contract Hepatitis C. In this way, generational trauma is not only transmitted but also propagated.

Generational trauma of slavery on African Americans

Systemic racism and discrimination are buzzwords in popular media and continue to be the topic of extensive study and debate. The Emancipation Proclamation t in America in 1865, did not immediately erase the trauma that slavery incurred. Dr. Alfiee Breland-Noble, director of the AAKOMA (African American Knowledge Optimized for Mindfully Healthy Adolescents) Project at Georgetown University has been exploring mental health disorders and treatments amongst African-Americans. She describes a "shared stress" experienced by African-Americans, claiming "there is a sense among African-Americans and other marginalized people that our stressors are unique to us and not necessarily shared by people outside our groups... so, we share stories of our lived experiences that help set the stage for how our loved ones encounter the world."

The public outrage spurred by the murder of George Floyd has made the issues faced by African-Americans in the United States particularly visible. Breland-Noble suggests that one of the challenges African-American parents face is talking with their children about potential police encounters stating that "It's traumatizing for parents and it's traumatizing for kids." Furthermore, she asserts that these experiences foster a sense of general distrust towards those outside of the African-American community. She describes how historically oppressive groups can be viewed in negative ways and how echo chambers and groupthink can further alienate these communities from one another.

Williams et al. has been working to further understand the sources and attitudes surrounding racial discrimination (6). In one study, the research group enrolled 123 African-American students who took an anxiety assessment tool. The results showed that those students who had high rates of perceived discrimination also had higher rates than others of uncontrollable paranoia, feelings of alienation, worries about future negative events and a perception that others were dangerous. While it is difficult to ascertain causal relationships, these correlations that were reported further support the notion that generational trauma can have repercussions that are far more complex and far-reaching than what is apparent at a surface level.

Closing Thoughts

In conclusion, generational trauma represents a term that is still shrouded in mystery. While psychologists, historians, anthropologists, and other scientists have been working to study and quantify this trauma, it is difficult to track or monitor precisely because trauma, like other psychological phenomena, could be silent or covert. In this section, we considered broadly what generational trauma is, but in subsequent chapters, we will consider the ways in which generational trauma can be inherited. Particularly, we will consider how trauma affects genetic processes, leading to traumatic reactivity and predispositions in those populations who are at greater risk.

Chapter 2: What is the Study of Epigenetics?

Peter Anto Johnson

Definition

Epigenetics is the study of the way in which your environment influences the mechanism by which your genes are read and translated. In contrast to genetic changes, epigenetic changes are reversible and can be modified. as it relates to how your genetic code is read as opposed to what your genetic code consists of.

Your genetic code consists of a sequence of nucleotides arranged in a predetermined order as determined by your genome and a multitude of other internal and external factors. One's epigenetics, on the other hand, involve functional changes which can impact how the genetic code is read, interpreted, and expressed without altering the sequence of nucleotides. Examples of these changes include DNA methylation, including cytosine methylation and hydroxymethylation, mRNA modifications, and histone modifications, which include lysine acetylation, lysine and arginine methylation, serine and threonine phosphorylation, and lysine ubiquitination and sumoylation.

Two classes of epigenetics exist: developmental and probabilistic. Developmental epigenesis relies on programming during embryonic or fetal development, where the growth trajectories are changed or impacted resulting in the adult phenotype, which is the development of certain genetically coded traits. On the other hand, probabilistic epigenesis depends entirely on the environment and individual experience and how it influences or interacts with the genetic code.

There are numerous mechanisms of developmental epigenetics, and the field itself continues to accumulate more research in a growing body of literature. A clinical vignette that portrays the importance of developmental epigenetics can be seen when we consider the effects of air pollution. In fact, it has been proposed that damage to DNA repair pathways might play a critical role in development of certain cancers, or carcinogenesis. Particularly, exposure to air pollution during pregnancy has a notable influence on placental mutation rate and DNA methylation of key repair genes. Previous studies have used advanced sequencing technology, which uses methods such as pyrosequencing, to investigate mutations and methylations and compare these with residential addresses, in order to compare air pollution and particulate matter exposure (Neven et al., 2018; Rider & Carlsten, 2019; Prunicki et al., 2021). These studies have determined prenatal exposure to air pollution was associated with higher placental mutation rate and epigenetic alterations, suggesting air pollution can induce changes to DNA repair capacity during the embryonic or fetal period.

An example of probabilistic epigenetics can be observed in several psychiatric conditions. Many of these conditions are explained by the diathesis stress model - a theory speculating there is an interaction between genetics and environment, where environmental stressors can predispose the individual to developing certain conditions. In particular, psychological insults in the environment such as a loss, grievance, harsh childhood experiences, or traumatic life events have been shown to increase the risk of bipolar disorder development and a number of associated psychiatric conditions. A similar example of this can be seen with alcohol and substance-use disorders, where early exposure to the substance can predispose the individual to developing an addiction or disorder.

History of study

Over the years, the study of epigenetics has evolved significantly (Felsenfeld, 2014). Traditionally, epigenetics was a term used to describe the rather poorly characterized process for the development of a fertilized zygote into a full organism. In fact, the concept of epigenesis emerged as an element of argument in the scientific community about the individual compartments that functioned as machinery in the cells of an organism to execute the genetically-coded events of development. Within this heated debate, two branches of thought have surfaced: the preformationism and epigenesis theories. The former believed that cells were already composed of preformed compartments that expand during development, whereas the latter maintained the process was one characterized by chemical synthesis reactions between soluble compartments, which directed the genetically coded events of development.

In the late 1870s, when chromosomes were identified as the site containing the genetic code , the epigenesis hypothesis gained much support. However, questions still remained (Felsenfeld, 2014). For instance, what these components were and how they reacted were still unknown. It was only in the 1930s that H. J. Muller first identified mutants in the fruit fly or Drosophila genome where the genetic components of chromatin appeared to be the same, but were different in the arrangement of their components (i.e., the nucleotides) (Muller, 1930). With much more evidence accumulating in a number of laboratories, the concept of chromosomal rearrangement and transposable elements that could alter the genetic code became clearer (Felsenfield, 2014).

From then onwards, there has been a great deal of interest and heated debate regarding the mechanisms of genetic code alterations, notably in cell structures such as the nucleus and cytoplasm during development. In contrast, the concept of probabilistic epigenesis and the ability of the genetic code to be altered in postnatal life is a concept that has only emerged in the 21st century (Valsiner, 2007). Regardless, much research about developmental and probabilistic epigenesis is still needed to understand the mechanisms of epigenetic change..

Clinical Significance

The importance of developmental epigenesis can be observed in the context of specific events during embryonic and fetal development (Jarrell et al., 2019). Consider fluid forces in embryonic heart development. A growing body of clinical and experimental evidence has shown abnormal epigenetic patterns in patients with a number of diseases such as congenital heart disease (CHD). Moreover, it is important to recognize mechanical forces which are essential elements for heart development. Blood flow directs the proper development of the heart, and in its absence, a variety of cardiac malformations can result. Much of the research has examined mechanical sensing mechanisms that are critical for governing cardiac development and epigenetic modifiers, which have also been suggested to have a crucial regulatory role in flow-dependent signaling mechanisms (Freund et al., 2012; Boselli et al., 2017).

Although implications of microscopic fluid forces in the human system have gained much interest over the recent years, little has been understood about its role during the development of the embryonic heart. Before Boselli et al. (2017) established that anisotropic shear stress patterns could be used to predict cardiac tissue movements in the embryo, it was unclear how spatial changes and fluid dynamics in tissues could play a role in cellular responses and behaviors. In their review, while Freund et al. (2012) present an appreciation for the role of shear stress and complex biophysics surrounding fluid flow dynamics, they recognize their incomplete understanding of the responses of endocardial cells leading to morphogenetic events in the heart, particularly valve formation. It explores how the heart was considered to respond to flow in a more sensitive fashion than other embryonic tissue systems which were considered, such as the left-right organizer, which senses cilia-mediated flow and is insensitive to geometric details. It also suggests the importance of positioning developing valves in contact with reversing flows for normal development. However, the contributions to endothelial cell migration from the mechanical forces resulting from this flow, namely shear stress, had yet to be identified.

In the study conducted by Boselli et al. (2017), the major aim was to identify the responses of endocardial cells to shear stress patterns during development. A secondary question that arises is how the cellular mechanism by which endocardial cells act, functions to produce this response. In addition, the authors also aimed to advance knowledge about the spatial and temporal profile of shear stress by considering a novel and simplified model that accounts for in vivo variables and takes into consideration the developing heart's sensitivity to geometric details in detecting blood flow.

Another example elucidating the significance of developmental and probabilistic epigenetics is evident when trying to understand the effects of sunshine-mediated effects during pregnancy on the offspring (Johnson & Johnson, 2020). Consider the association between ultraviolet (UV) light exposure by pregnant women and the incidence of multiple sclerosis (MS) in their children. In a longitudinal study conducted by Staples et al. (2010) in 1,524 participants identified an Australian birth registration database, lower exposures to ambient UV during the first trimester of pregnancy was associated with an increased risk of MS in offspring. It has been suggested vitamin D may be implicated in genetic mechanisms, which increase interactions with a locus determining susceptibility to MS. Therefore, stressors in later life may lead to the development of MS in these populations.

MS was also studied by Vio Streym et al (2013), who used the national register database to identify birth cohorts in Denmark to identify associations between seasonal exposures and long-term conditions including MS, type 1 diabetes, cancer, schizophrenia, ischemic heart disease, and pneumonia. MS and pneumonia in the young subjects was significantly dependent on season of birth, and thus maternal vitamin D exposure, suggesting low sunlight exposure in the winter resulted in a higher incidence of MS and pneumonia in infants (Johnson & Johnson, 2020).

Another prospective cohort study conducted by Sayers and Tobias (2009) suggested UV-B exposure is connected to skeletal development in offspring. This study examined 6995 children in a Finnish cohort after considering UV-B exposure in the third trimester of pregnancy based on meteorological monitoring data showing a relationship with bone mass and size in later childhood. This suggested vitamin D status in pregnancy has direct effects on programming periosteal bone formation. though adjustments were not made for environmental, genetic or social factors.

The reviewed literature suggests UV exposure is key for different windows of vulnerability throughout fetal development (Johnson & Johnson, 2020). Its effects in the first trimester are suggested by Tustin et al (2004) and Staples et al (2010), where vitamin D could play an integral role in early fetal development. Sayers and Tobias (2009) further considers its effects in the third trimester, when skeletal development events are occurring in the fetus and the presence of UV-induced maternal vitamin D could be required. A need for UV-induced vitamin D during developmental events, such as reduced risk of MS, in formation of the nervous system in the first trimester. Alternatively, it may lower risk of pneumonia, which could involve events in the third trimester during lung development, and may explain reported outcomes. Lastly larger birthweight outcomes could also suggest UV-induced vitamin D is implicated in normal fetal growth (Johnson & Johnson, 2020).

From this clinical overview, it is easy for us to recognize that epigenetic modifications such as DNA methylation, histone modifications and non-coding RNAs could all be implicated in determining how an offspring's early life environment could have long-lasting effects on health in later life (Bianco-Miotto et al., 2017; Johnson & Johnson, 2020). Similarly, we can understand epigenetics can have an exacerbated effects on vulnerable populations, which becomes essential when we consider our discussion of generational trauma. A sustained disparity exists among already vulnerable groups owing to inherent systemic flaws already present in society, healthcare, and other domains due to a number of factors including socioeconomics, cultural variables, and genetics.

The long-standing effects of epigenetics and intergenerational trauma are evident in Canada's Indigenous populations and healthcare systems. While certain definitive health statements about the relationship between COVID-19 and other health conditions cannot be made as of the publishing of this book, the novel coronavirus pandemic has been found to impact the health-compromised to a greater extent, a large proportion of whom are Indigenous. Therefore, it has been speculated that Indigenous communities will be more severely affected by COVID-19. Both rural- and urban-located Indigenous persons have unique physical and mental health risks, whether resulting from environmental exposures within their own lifetime or passed down through genetics. Physical conditions include tuberculosis, type 2 diabetes, obesity, and kidney disease, and mental conditions include severe depression, substance abuse disorders and intergenerational trauma

(Aboriginal Healing Foundation, 2003). Despite having unique health risks, healthcare is often very difficult for Indigenous persons - especially those living in remote communities - to access.

Many chronic health conditions plaguing Canada's Indigenous population today can be traced back to residential schools, where children were often severely malnourished (Mosby and Galloway, 2017). Chronic caloric intake restrictions cause permanent physical damage, often leading to stunted growth and a decreased metabolic rate. This decreased metabolic rate results in a greater accumulation of fat tissue in place of muscle mass increase, thereby increasing the likelihood of obesity later in life. Another effect of malnutrition is a decrease in insulin levels, leading to a prevalence in the development of type 2 diabetes. As the physical and mental health impacts of the residential school system are ongoing, the residential school experience is still very relevant today. Studies have shown that the health conditions developed by women who were chronically malnourished can result in negative health effects at birth in their children, and are subsequently passed on to their children's children as well. Thus, the implications of residential schools are multigenerational.

Chapter 3: How did we come to understand the link between epigenetics and generational trauma?

Alyssa Wu

Introduction to Epigenetics and Generational Trauma

The study of epigenetics looks at changes experienced at the level of molecular genetics, including the mutations and alterations of DNA that consequently affect our genome. Each individual has a unique genetic fingerprint, making us distinct compared to our peers. Genetic variations are responsible for our overall physiology, pathology, and phenotypic traits (including eye colour, hair colour, weight, and height). It has long been believed that variations in our DNA are responsible for changing our genetic code. However, current research is showing that experiences can shape our behaviour (Shadows of the Past, n.d.). This is a complex topic within biology and psychology, known as the "nature vs. nurture debate". It has been argued that since "epigenetic events happen at the interface between DNA and its environment, they can help us to see how our features always arise from both nature and nurture" (Witherington & Lickliter, 2017). The nature vs. nurture debate has been discussed for long periods of time throughout various fields of study, including epigenetics, evolutionary and biological sciences, and psychology. These classification systems have drawn a divide between the systems of inheritance, as we understand these concepts today. However, many authors have argued that there are "genetic, epigenetic and exogenetic resources, but none of them can be identified by a single role in development or a unique way of transgenerational transmission" (Stotz & Griffiths, 2016).

The environment can majorly impact the human body, which can lead to an individual experiencing a wide range of traumatic events. Trauma can be categorized into three main types: acute, chronic, and complex traumas. Acute trauma is typically the result of a single distressing event to an individual, which may have affected a person's emotional or physical security. The after-effects associated with acute trauma could be exhibited in many ways, including "excessive anxiety or panic, irritation, confusion, inability to have a restful sleep, feelings of disconnection from the surrounding, unreasonable lack of trust, inability to focus on work or studies, lack of self-care or grooming, [and/or] aggressive behaviour" (Allarakha & Suyog Uttekar, 2021). Chronic trauma usually stems from personal exposure to prolonged periods of distress. Multiple cases of untreated or unattended acute traumas can lead and progress into chronic trauma. Symptoms of chronic trauma are typically experienced years after the event and can result in "labile or unpredictable emotional outbursts, anxiety, extreme anger, flashbacks, fatigue, body aches, headaches, and nausea" (Allarakha & Suyog Uttekar, 2021). People experience complex trauma when they have been exposed to multiple trauma experiences that are varied in nature. Complex trauma can affect many areas of a person's life, including "overall health, relationships, and performance at work or school" (Allarakha & Suyog Uttekar, 2021).

The Impact on the Holocaust and American Civil War

The phenomenon of understanding the associations between generational trauma and epigenetics can be better understood through examining case studies involved the children of the Holocaust survivors, as well as the former prisoners of war from the American Civil War. The children of the Holocaust survivors were left with epigenetically marked chromosomes. There is a chemical coating that holds some biological memory of what the parents experienced. According to the adaptations made in response to environmental factors, this memory holds a general vulnerability to stress and resilience factors. It was determined that "epigenetics may explain why latent transmission becomes manifest under stress" (Kellermann, 2013). Characteristics of Holocaust survivors include higher mortality rates and increased stress levels. These experiences can influence "gene expression, creating distinct epigenetic signatures that negatively impact life expectancy, mental health, behaviour, and more" (Shadows of the Past, n.d.).

During the American Civil War, it was found that there are long-term effects on the sons of the former prisoners of war. These men were very susceptible to disease, stress, and psychological stress, as they lived in very poor environmental conditions. Later studies confirmed that these men experienced decreasing health status, employment barriers and a shortened life span. A study done by the researchers at the University of California, Los Angeles (UCLA) examined the life expectancy rates of the sons from the former prisoners of war. They found that the sons also experience higher mortality rates compared to the general population. These researchers made the association that "it seemed as if their sons were also affected by the trauma they had experienced" (Shadows of the Past, n.d.).

Further study has found that the epigenetics of inherited trauma tends to affect more men than women. This is known as the Father-Son Phenomenon (Shadows of the Past, n.d.). There is an epigenetic effect that is found on the Y chromosome in males. In 2016, it was observed that DNA methylation patterns on the Y chromosome are more stable than X chromosomes, which leads to the hypothesis that this association translates into stronger epigenetic action (Shadows of the Past, n.d.). Another research study suggests that epigenetic trauma is more readily passed down from the fathers to their sons. By studying the effects of food shortages in remote Swedish villages, they found that "the consequences of improper nutrition were only transmitted down the male line of descendants" (Shadows of the Past, n.d.).

Human Genome Project

The study of epigenetics has become increasingly prominent in stabilizing alterations to the genome and histone proteins that are responsible for gene expression. Disruptions to these expression patterns are very common in certain types of hereditary cancers, including breast cancer, leukemia, lymphoma, ovarian cancer, prostate cancer, skin cancers, and thyroid cancers (Canadian Cancer Society, n.d.). Epigenetic changes affect disease risk, stress response and metabolism. There are both positive and negative changes to the epigenetic code when they are implemented in the genome. For example, some alterations can make a patient more susceptible to cancer and neuropsychiatric disorders.

Another example of a disease that can be caused by epigenetic alterations is the detrimental effects of traumatic stress or drug/toxic exposure on brain functions. The study of epigenetics aims to describe reversible genome modifications that are meiotically and mitotically heritable (Tammen et al., 2013).

The Human Epigenome Project is an extension of the Human Genome Project, which started in October 1990 and was completed in April 2003 (The Human Genome Project, n.d.). The main goal of the Human Genome Project is to sequence and map all of the genes in the human genome. Using the information revealed by the Human Genome Project, epigenetic advancements are now possible and researchers will be able to use this information to elucidate more accurate results. Current research is looking at studying the defects that are associated with epigenetic regulation. These processes include imprinting, X chromosome activation, transcriptional control of genes, and mutations that affect DNA methylation enzymes. These mechanisms all contribute to the etiology and pathology of human disease. The goal of the Human Epigenome Project is to identify, catalog and interpret genome-wide DNA methylation patterns of all human genes in all major tissues (Eckhardt et al., 2004).

Histone modifications are very common in epigenetic-related research. The DNA is supercoiled and compacted very tightly around histone problems. This forms DNA-protein complexes, known as nucleosomes. Within these histone modifications, many post-translational modifications are implemented on the N-terminal histone tails of the DNA that help facilitate histone packaging in mammalian cells. These processes include "histone acetylation, methylation, phosphorylation, ubiquitination, ADP-ribosylation, and biotinylation" (Tammen et al., 2013). Post-translational modifications affect the structure and function of histone modifications. These histone modifications can help in the regulation of chromatin, which is a DNA scaffold complex that contains instructions that respond to the external cues that are encoded by the DNA biological material. For example, a research study conducted in 1964 showed that histone acetylation of lysines is "highly dynamic and regulated by the opposing action of two families of enzymes, histone acetyltransferases (HATs) and histone deacetylases (HDACs)" (Bannister & Kouzarides, 2011). Histone phosphorylation typically occurs on serines, threonines, and tyrosines on the N-terminal histone tails. These modifications are controlled by the action of kinase enzymes, which add modifications, whereas phosphatase enzymes remove modifications (Bannister & Kouzarides, 2011).

DNA methylation is continuing to be a very well-studied mechanism of epigenetic change that affects the biological functioning of an organism. DNA methylation is a natural process that occurs in aging. Methylation can also be induced by cancerous cells, which creates aberrations in methylated genes. It has been found that specific regions of methylation changes have been associated with decreased organ function, memory, bone density, and other age-related health problems (Tammen et al., 2013). The process of histone methylation adds or removes chemical tags that are found within a DNA sequence. These modifications are typically found on the side chains of lysines and arginines. However, it is important to note that, unlike histone acetylation and phosphorylation, methylation does not alter the charge of the compact histone protein (Bannister & Kouzarides, 2011). The purpose of these chemical tags is to mark specific genes or signalling sequences that need to be turned on or off to support proper genetic functioning within a cell. As there are alot of genes that need to be accounted for within a cell, methylation acts as a filtering process that shows the cell which genes are critical for functioning, and which ones can be overlooked. This characteristic of methylating important gene sequences allows the cell to adapt to their changing environmental conditions without permanently shifting their DNA patterns and structures (Shadows of the Past, n.d.). It has been found that methylated positions within the genome reflect the level of gene activity, as well as the type and disease state of a cell or tissue. These epigenetic markers are key tools with many features that reveal the ever-changing dynamic state of the genome (Eckhardt et al., 2004).

Understanding the Implications of Inherited Trauma

Studies have shown that there are large impacts on the science of inheritance leading to implications of inherited trauma through the study of epigenetics. Generational trauma can be passed on from the adult to the child, which can affect the way than an individual views and perceives traumatic events. Human experiences are shaped by contextual perspectives that influence the way we view the world. As human brains and thought processes are very complex, our experiences are also shaped by understanding the legacies that our ancestors left behind. Generational trauma and disease inheritance patterns have been observed in a wide variety of organisms, many of which have connections to different levels of exposure to environmental triggers. An early study has found that environmental toxins, such as fungicides and pesticides, promote the epigenetic transgenerational inheritance of reproductive disease. Environmental factors and nutritional abnormalities such as caloric restrictions and high-fat diets can increase the likelihood of adopting a transgenerational disease. Other toxins that can make individuals susceptible to disease include plastics, dioxin, biocides, dichlorodiphenyltrichloroethane (DDT), and hydrocarbons (Skinner, 2014).

However, despite these motives, there are still many unexplained mysteries of human resilience. For example, why do some children thrive, while others don't? Why do certain groups of people experience higher mortality rates? And are we irrevocably bound to the past? Examining the answers to these questions in depth will help healthcare professionals better reclassify genetic disorders. This knowledge can be passed on to other scientists, clinicians, mental health practitioners, and other specialists as well (Shadows of the Past, n.d.). Improving our current reclassification system for genetic disorders can help ameliorate preventative and post-exposure treatment methods for patient populations who are vulnerable, susceptible, or currently suffer from the manifestation of trauma. This includes developing a better understanding on the effects of malnutrition or starvation, creating stronger treatment plans for post-traumatic stress disorder (PTSD) and other mental health disorders, increasing access to medical care in affected populations, and preventing abuse, neglect, familial separation, and other events known to trigger adverse epigenetic effects (Shadows of the Past, n.d.).

Conclusion

As scientists unravel more mysteries surrounding the associations between epigenetics and generational trauma, other healthcare professionals can learn and better understand how to diagnose patients correctly. Research has shown that traumatic experiences that were experienced by our ancestors can be passed down through our genetic material. This newly found discovery will allow clinicians to better understand the patient history and avoid misdiagnosing patients. Further research will look into expanding on the knowledge that scientists currently understand linking the associations and connections between generational trauma and epigenetics. Similar to single nucleotide polymorphisms and methylation variable positions, these tools will be fundamental in building our understanding to better understand and diagnose the molecular basis of human disease.

Chapter 4: How do we study Epigenetics?
Rushmi Jamil

Introduction

Epigenetics involves the study of processes that can cause heritable genetic changes which are not a result of mutations in the DNA sequence itself but still affect genetic activity and protein translation, such as DNA methylation or histone modification. These changes affect the chromatin structure, which in turn has an impact on gene expression. These changes are studied using molecular biology techniques such as x, x, x.. Forms of epigenetic modifications include methylation, acetylation, phosphorylation, ubiquitylation, and sumoylation (Weinhold, 2006). DNA methylation is the most prevalent form of epigenetic modification, in which a methyl group is added to or removed from a region of consecutive cytosine bases.

DNA methylation has been observed to have adverse effects and has been linked to diseases such as cancer. Histones, proteins that are present in chromatin and play an important role in DNA stability and expression, can themselves be modified in another form of epigenetic change, which occurs through histone acetylation, methylation or ubiquitination. In either scenario, the main approach to study epigenetic changes involves identifying where and what kind of changes have occurred, followed by an assessment of how those changes translate to macroscale biology. This chapter discusses some of the techniques that have been used to identify such changes, with a nod to the rapid advancements in technology which mean these techniques are constantly improving.

Chromatin modification analysis

Epigenetic modification of DNA or histones ultimately results in changes to the chromatin structure. Chromatin is made up of condensed nucleosomes that are packed together. Histones play an important role in the formation of chromatins, and therefore an alteration in the histone structure can result in changes in the chromatin structure as well. Changes in the chromatin structure affect gene expression, since the availability of different genes for transcription changes as the chromatin coils to cover or uncover different strands of DNA. Chromatin accessibility analysis is a broad technique used to directly measure which regions of DNA are accessible in chromatin. The first step involves cross-linking chromatin-bound proteins using formaldehyde, followed by enzymatic digestion of larger DNA strands into smaller chunks. This is achieved through nucleases, which are enzymes that break down nucleic acid chains into their respective monomers. Nucleases cannot access regions of chromatin that are blocked, and so once the remaining DNA sequences can be amplified using qPCR (quantitative polymerase chain reaction), a method that is commonly used in studying gene expression, the sites of DNA which are rendered inaccessible by the chromatin remodeling can be identified. At this stage, chromatin immunoprecipitation (ChIP) can be used to precipitate DNA strands of interest. The technique involves introducing antibodies that bind to proteins on the DNA (Das et al., 2004). Next-generation sequencing (NGS) can be used to determine the roles of the genes hidden by the chromatin. Of particular interest are genes that might have been involved in coding for the chromatin condensation, such as silencers or insulators (Song & Crawford, 2010). Deoxyribonuclease I (DNase I) is an example of an endonuclease that can digest single or double stranded DNA.

Chromosome Conformation Capture (3C) is a method of studying genomic organization within living organisms at a scale of a few tens to hundreds of kilobase-pairs (Hagège et al., 2007). Studying the folding of the genome at a macro- scale allows us to identify regions that are involved in gene regulation. The method also provides insight on the 3D structure of chromatin. 3C also involves the use of formaldehyde to cross-link proteins in the cells, 'fixating' them and preserving their in-vivo structure so that they can be studied. Chromatins are then isolated and subjected to digestion using a restriction enzyme such as an endonuclease. The enzymes are chosen according to the sequence of DNA that is being targeted, as many nucleases only cleave DNA at specific base-pair sequences. The resultant sections of DNA are joined into rings and the crosslinks are reversed (). Quantitative PCR is then used to determine the abundance of the target sequence in the purified DNA. In epigenetic studies, 3C can be used to identify conformational changes in chromatins, and alterations in genomic regions that affect gene expression. The 3C technique has been further streamlined for advanced epigenetic analyses: circular chromosome conformation capture (4C) allows us to investigate the interactions between genetic loci, while Chromosome Conformation Capture Carbon Copy (5C) allows us to analyse genomic interactions by implementing next generation sequencing technologies to identify neighbouring DNA regions in vivo (Dostie et al., 2006).

Fluorescence in-situ hybridization (FISH) is a method that utilizes the complementary nature of DNA strands to identify molecules in chromatins. Fluorophore-coupled nucleotides are introduced to selected single DNA strands in order to determine whether complementary sequences are present in the strands (Cui, Shu & Li, 2016). If binding between the fluorescent probes and the DNA strands occur, the complementary regions can be examined using fluorescence imaging techniques, as the fluorescence signal is enhanced upon successfully binding to DNA. FISH has many applications in molecular biology; however, in epigenetic studies, it can be used specifically to investigate chromosome structure, positioning, and gene expression, as well as to detect any chromosomal abnormalities.

Histone modification analysis

Histone modification occurs when molecules such as methyls, acetyls or ubiquitin bind to amino acids in the N-terminal regions (or tails) of histones. Although the full impact of histone modification is not yet known, it has been observed that it influences which regions of the genomic sequence are open for transcription, hence affecting gene expression. ChIP uses antibodies that target histones bound to chromatin. Thus, immunoprecipitation techniques can be used to identify histones bound to chromatin under different epigenetic scenarios. Mass spectrometry is commonly used to study histone modifications at a molecular level. Mass spectrometry necessitates the isolation of histones from the nucleus, which can be achieved relatively simply by acid treatment, as histones are basic. Controlled enzymatic digestion of the histones breaks the typically large proteins into chunks, facilitating part-by-part analysis of the larger histone. The actual data analysis involves shattering the protein fragments into molecular fragments and recording the nuclear mass of each fragment. If the peptide sequence of each fragment is known, the identity of histone modifications can be discerned by unexpected increases in the mass of a fragment (for example, a single methylation would increase the atomic mass by 19). A study was conducted in the University of Wisconsin-Madison in which all the histone modifications that occurred in the 23 residues of the N-terminal tail of the histone H4 in human embryonic stem cells were mapped and a helpful protocol is provided for general histone modification analysis.

DNA Methylation Analysis

DNA methylation is the process through which a methyl group is attached to a cytosine residue, converting the cytosine into 5-methylcytosine (5mC). Aside from gene expression, DNA methylation can also affect embryonic development, cellular proliferation, differentiation and chromosome stability (Li & Tollefsbol, 2011). It is therefore the most extensively studied form of epigenetic modification, and there are currently several methods that can be used to detect it. One of these methods is bisulfite sequencing, which involves treating the DNA sequence with sodium bisulfite. This causes unmethylated cytosines in single-stranded DNA to become converted into uracil residues, while 5mCs remain unchanged, allowing us to differentiate between methylated and unmethylated cytosines. This is followed by the addition of primers that are complementary to the bisulfite-converted sequences. The DNA is then amplified through PCR and purified before it is analyzed through sequencing. In the sequencing stage, un-methylated cytosines are replaced by thymine, while methylated cytosines remain (Hashimoto et al., 2007). Treatment with sodium bisulfite combined with PCR and DNA sequencing can therefore be used to determine whether specific sections of DNA are methylated.

Another method of detecting DNA methylation is through the use of methylation-sensitive restriction enzymes (MSRE). A CpG site is a section of DNA in which a cytosine nucleotide is followed by a guanine nucleotide. When the cytosine in a CpG site is not methylated, the MSREs are able to cut the DNA strand at that point. Methylated CpG sites however cannot be cleaved and are therefore amplified when subjected to PCR. The presence of PCR strands therefore serves as an indicator of the presence of methylated CpG sites in a region of DNA. The MSRE must be selected according to the recognition sites present in the target DNA sequence (Hashimoto et al., 2007). This method of detecting methylation in DNA is very simple, since it only requires the DNA sample to be digested by the selected MSRE, followed by PCR analysis.

Methylated DNA Immunoprecipitation (MeDIP) is a method of extracting methylated DNA from a prepared sample of DNA. It is essential for the sample DNA to be pure, meaning proteins such as histones cannot be present. The sample must also be treated to remove as much RNA as possible, since they can interfere in the binding of antibodies. The sample DNA is then fragmented through sonication, a process that involves subjecting the DNA to ultrasonic frequencies. Antibodies that bind to the methylated regions of the DNA sequence are then added to the sample. After incubating the DNA sample with a magnetic antibody, the methylated DNA is separated from the sample using magnets. Any non-methylated DNA is washed off using a buffer, and the antibody is cleaved using Proteinase K. The DNA sample is further purified using phenol chloroform, after which the methylated DNA and its properties can be further investigated (Thu et al., 2009).

High Resolution Melt analysis (HRM) is a technique used to determine the degree of methylation of DNA. To do this, DNA must be extracted from the nucleus, after which it is replicated using polymerase chain reaction (PCR) to provide an adequate quantity for analysis. The DNA is then treated with sodium bisulfite, which produces uracil from unmethylated cytosine residues. The DNA is then slowly frozen, and its temperature is monitored using high resolution thermometers. Methylated DNA contains less unmethylated cytosine compared to normal DNA, so will contain fewer impurities. This results in a higher, more constant melting point when compared to regular DNA. These differences in melting point indicate the degree of methylation of DNA.

DNA and protein interaction analysis

DNA and protein interaction is an integral part in the regulation of important cellular functions including gene transcription, DNA replication and recombination, repair, cell cycle progression, and epigenetic silencing (Das et al., 2018). Binding between histones, as well as other regulatory proteins, and DNA is what facilitates the 3D structure of chromatin. It is therefore worth investigating how DNA-binding proteins interact with the genomic sequence and identify which protein binds to which region in the DNA sequence in vivo. DNA-protein interaction studies investigate the way DNA interacts with proteins under a variety of conditions. Epigenetics uses these studies to determine how gene expression is altered by environmental factors, resulting in metabolic disorders that may lead to disease. Type 2 diabetes and cancer in particular are known to be influenced by environmental factors. Some epigenetic studies also investigate how drugs interact with DNA and how the interactions change due to methylation in an effort to find more efficient treatments (Liu, Li & Tollefsbol, 2008).

DNA adenine methyltransferase identification (DamID) assay is a method that can be used to detect local and genome-wide DNA-protein interactions, using a fusion protein that contains the protein of interest and E. coli DNA adenine methyltransferase. This fusion protein can methylate the adenine base near protein-DNA interaction sites. The Adenine-methylated DNA strands can then be replicated and detected using PCR analysis (Wu, Olson & Yao, 2016).

Another method of detecting DNA-protein interaction is through chromatin immunoprecipitation (ChIP). ChIP can be used to detect the location of binding of transcription factors, histones and other proteins in vivo. Chromatin-protein complexes are first fixated using formaldehyde, in order to preserve their in-vivo conformation. They are then fragmented using sonication or a DNA nuclease. The DNA-binding protein of interest then undergoes immunoprecipitation using specific antibodies. The DNA is then uncoupled from the proteins and analyzed using various methods, such as PCR, qPCR, sequencing, and microarray hybridization, which yields high-resolution sequences of the protein-binding sites. Using ChIP in combination with techniques such as parallel sequencing (ChIP-seq), allows us to identify binding sites of the proteins of interest, and can reveal all the binding sites for a given protein not only locally but throughout the entire genome.

Computational Analysis of Epigenetics

Over the last two decades a wealth of data has emerged through databases, and the ability to analyze these datasets through computational tools has resulted in a deeper understanding of the human genome as well as gene factors and expression. However, it has also become increasingly evident that mutations in DNA sequence are not enough to explain the diversity and heritable changes in phenotype. This has driven the need to understand epigenetic processes and their impact on the human genome, as well as their influence in certain diseases such as cancer, obesity, heart disease and diabetes (Ruskin & Barat, 2021). Recent research has also suggested there may be a link between epigenetic or environmental factors and neuropsychiatric disorders. The Epigenomics Road Map is a monumental project that aims to produce a map of the epigenome of various tissue types and cancers, alongside investigating specific epigenetic processes. Computational tools for analyzing such large datasets require an interdisciplinary approach that combines principles of biochemistry, mathematics, computer science, and other physical sciences. One of the primary goals of using computational analysis for epigenetic research is to be able to model fundamental epigenetic processes such as DNA methylation and histone modification (Ruskin & Barat, 2021).

Conclusion

Epigenetic processes are heritable molecular changes that occur in the DNA sequence that do not alter the sequence itself. These changes can occur in DNA, through the addition or removal of certain chemical groups, or through modification of histones, proteins that facilitate DNA packaging. Both changes can result in alteration of the conformation of chromatins, which affects which regions of the gene sequence are accessible for transcription. Many well-established techniques to study DNA are relevant in the field of epigenetics, but increasing attention is being given toward computational techniques that can either be predictive or supplement experimental techniques. Epigenetics is inherently an extremely vast field of study, which lends itself to the iterative improvement of the techniques used to understand it.

Chapter 5: How do we study Generational Trauma?

Rushmi Jamil

Introduction

Since the conception of the study of generational trauma in 1966, many studies were conducted that investigated the effect of this trauma on the children of Holocaust survivors (Sigal & Rakoff, 1971). The implications of generational trauma are far reaching, since it means that any kind of prolonged emotional or psychological trauma can affect not only an individual but also future generations. Generational trauma often manifests as hypervigilance, mistrust, high anxiety, depression, panic attacks, nightmares, insomnia and issues with self-esteem and self-confidence. Some studies suggest that an extended period of trauma can damage nerve endings in the brain, which can result in genetic changes that may be inherited by future generations (Gillespie, 2020). It is difficult to diagnose generational trauma since it can result in a complex mixture of behavioural and physiological complications. Despite the widespread interest in generational trauma and the numerous studies that have been conducted on this subject, it is still a relatively new field of study, and much remains unknown at present. This chapter discusses the various ways in which generational trauma has been studied and what information has been discovered through each of these approaches. The use of method should be guided by hypothesis and curated based on the type of trauma being assessed.

Sociology

A study conducted in 1999 found that second generation Vietnamese immigrants in the United States had higher levels of mental distress in comparison to first generation immigrants. The study focused on analyzing the psychosocial adaptation of three generations of Vietnamese immigrants (Shapiro et al., 1999). In addition, they attempted to identify possible predictors of psychological distress among the Vietnamese immigrant community. A group of 184 Vietnamese immigrants took part in the study as a sample group. The age of participants ranged from youth to elderly adults. The study examined their mental state such as levels of anxiety, depression, and PTSD, but also psychosocial aspects of their lives such as family conflict, dissatisfaction with life in the U.S., acculturation and biculturalism, social support, coping, and pre-migratory stress factors. Young adults, despite being the least depressed, reported feeling the most dissatisfied with their lives in the US, and faced the most family conflict regardless of their higher family income. It was determined that their distress stemmed from increased acculturation and difficulty in adjusting to life in the US, as well as increased conflict with their families.

A sociological perspective facilitates discussion of wider societies, extrapolating data gathered from individual families to understand the Vietnamese immigrant community at large. Some studies examine the transference of trauma between generations through an attachment theory perspective. Attachment theory proposes that the bond between a parent and their infant is integral in the development of the child's sense of self as well as their understanding of others (Cassidy, Jones & Shaver, 2003). According to this theory, a disruption in this relationship can result in behavioural problems in the children as adults, and subjects them to a sense of intense anxiety and loss. A study conducted by Zeanah and Zeanah in 1989 found that adults characterized as 'preoccupied' were less able to organize their internal emotions and were less capable of resolving personal issues, often resulting in a parent-child relationship that was insecure (Doucet & Rovers, 2010). Doucet and Rovers therefore suggested that generational trauma may be the result of such parent-child relationships, where a parent, having gone through some traumatic event such as separation from their own parents, is unable to form a healthy relationship with their own children. Doucet and Rovers also suggest that parents' unresolved emotions regarding traumatic experiences may lead to disorganization and confusion in a parent-child relationship. Another study by Lev-Wiesel in 2007 found that second and third generation children of Holocaust survivors tend to overidentify with their parents or their grandparents' traumatic experiences, and have a heightened sense of their status as Holocaust survivors. It was found that children must often assume a role of responsibility that is beyond them, resulting in their 'parentification'. They also tend to mistrust and fear other people in general. These behavioural manifestations of intergenerational trauma were explained by Doucet and Rovers as a result of children having to bear the burden of their parents unresolved emotional trauma (Doucet & Rovers, 2010).

Psychology

Generational trauma can also be studied through investigating the effect the traumatic experiences of previous generations have on the psychology and behaviour of future generations. Examination of the psychological state of first-generation Holocaust survivors has shown that they suffer from high levels of psychological and emotional distress and exhibit posttraumatic symptoms which can later manifest in their children as well. A study conducted by Fossion et. al. in 2003 found that the children of Holocaust survivors were highly susceptible to developing post-traumatic stress disorder (PTSD). The study also found that the children of Holocaust survivors tend to aim towards overachieving in order to compensate for their parents' loss. It was found that third-generation Holocaust survivors were thrice as likely to seek psychiatric help compared to the general population. The psychological lens clarifies how trauma manifests across generations, drawing on the rich literature on psychological trauma to understand the relatively younger field of generational trauma.

A study by Motta et al. (1997) presented evidence of the transmission of trauma from parents to their children by comparing the results of a modified Stroop test taken by the children of war veterans and children of non-veterans. The Stroop test is a neuropsychological test that examines an individual's ability to process multiple stimuli at once. Using a modified version of a standard test to detect secondary trauma provides a means of identifying generational trauma that is less prone to misdiagnosis, which is present in methods such as interviewing survivors and their children, due to subjective interpretation. The modified test used in the study utilized cards with neutral and war-related words printed in different colours. Similar to the original test, participants were asked to name the color of the word while ignoring the word itself. The study found that children of war veterans had a delay in processing the colour of war-related words, compared to the children of non-veterans. This method is therefore able to detect subtle influences of trauma on the psychology of future generations that may simply be present in their subconscious mind. This modified Stroop test can therefore help diagnose individuals who are not aware that they are psychologically or emotionally affected by secondary trauma.

History

Generational trauma can also be studied by examining the socio-economical and psychological condition of current generations of historically oppressed communities. It was reported that non-Hispanic Native Americans are at high risk of experiencing psychological distress, with suicide being the second leading cause of death among Native Americans between the ages of 10-34 (Brown-Rice, 2013). Native Americans were subjected to a systematic destruction of their culture and people at the hands of colonizers. Their loss of land, people, family and culture over the last 500 years have resulted in traumatic experiences that have affected many generations of Native Americans. This has led to feelings of loss, shame, powerlessness and subordination among the Native American community. The socio-economic, psychological and physiological difficulties faced by Native Americans today may be a direct result of their historical trauma (Brown-Rice, 2013). Psychological concerns among the current Native American population includes increased alcohol consumption, substance abuse and mental health disorders. Abuse of alcohol by Native individuals may be related to 'low self-esteem, loss of cultural identity, lack of positive role models, history of abuse and neglect, self-medication due to feelings of hopelessness, and loss of family and tribal connections' (Brown-Rice, 2013).

A study involving three generations of the survivors of the Holodomor, an event in which Soviet Ukrainians were subjected to mass starvation during the regime of Joseph Stalin, showed that there was indeed a transgenerational transmission of the horrific event (Bezo & Maggi, 2015). The children and grandchildren of survivors learned from previous generations to have a general wariness of the world and people in it. Many claimed to live in 'survival mode', relying solely on oneself and lacking a sense of community. Current generations also indulge in risky health behaviors such as food hoarding and overeating, which have a direct relation to their traumatic past. They also reported experiencing feelings of shame and anxiety. Some also develop authoritarian parenting styles and have reported an excessive emotional dependency of parents on their children (Bezo & Maggi, 2015). These findings are consistent with the studies on the families of Holocaust survivors, the displacement of Native American Indians and the oppression of African Americans. The fact that all these communities have a history of traumatic experiences in common and have similar problems plaguing current generations serves as evidence that prolonged traumatic experiences influence the psychological, cultural, and potentially even the genetics of future generations.

Interviewing Survivors

A study of the grandchildren of Holocaust survivors published in 2003 extracted data from therapy sessions with families of Holocaust survivors (Fossion, 2003). While intergenerational trauma had been well-studied in the first-generation of Holocaust survivors and the second-generation, i.e., the children, of Holocaust survivors, the third-generation, or the grandchildren of Holocaust survivors, are a population whose trauma has been less documented. During the time of the study, this population was roughly adolescent. The specific manifestations of trauma in the third generation are distinct from both the first and second generations, and comprise of features such as academic issues, problems with substance abuse, and various psychological disorders. The study arose from a rise in the frequency of therapy sessions requested by survivor families, prompted by the problems faced by third-generation Holocaust survivors. With the premise of a familial root for their trauma, the clinical approach involved asking the younger population to consult with their grandparents to rationalize the familial procession of trauma. Interviews permitted the researchers to become very familiar with the specific circumstances of each patient. This can be a useful way to avoid false positives: the researchers in this study recognized that the problems faced by the patients could be explained by a variety of other identifiable factors during their therapy sessions.

Nirit Gradwohl Pisano, a third-generation Holocaust survivor herself, performed a survey of third-generation Holocaust survivors and published a book on her findings in 2012 (Pisano, 2012). She interviewed her peers who had volunteered to share their experiences with her. Nirit's brief explanation of her methodology highlights the strengths and weaknesses of interviewing as a means to assess generational trauma. As a topic that is inherently sensitive, many respondents may withdraw when asked to probe their subconscious trauma. A tactful interviewer asks nuanced questions to draw out relevant information. An interview also permits the interviewee to share whatever they feel is worth sharing in an open-ended manner, permitting a holistic understanding of the topic. Furthermore, the personal, one-on-one nature of the interview allows interpretations to be made from silence, as hesitation or reluctance can be viewed as demonstrations of generational trauma.

Population studies

. The method of population study stands distinct from the previously discussed methods of analyzing generational trauma, in that it specifically looks at properties shared by populations of interest, independent of the framework of some sociological or psychological theory. Population studies to understand generational trauma are very systematic and structured. Choice of population is key, as the group must be linked through the common experience of generational trauma. A modern suggestion is to include more extreme age ranges, especially when trying to understand generational trauma in children (Sangalang, 2017). This has two benefits: firstly, an adult speaking about their childhood experiences will relay the same information differently from a child; secondly, identifying and treating trauma appropriately prevents the adverse effects of the trauma influencing the child's adolescence and adulthood. One approach involves comparing a selected age group with existing literature that has examined trauma in older generations (Pisano, 2012). Other population studies will include members across generations and find contrasts among generations (West,

2012). The examples that follow highlight the ways in which this technique stands apart from the others, but it should be noted that all studies discussed so far are excellent examples of careful population selection and analysis.

A study born out of a desire to understand lower advance directive document completion rates among African Americans delved deep into the attitudes towards the US healthcare system across generations (West, 2012). The population selected for this study included African American attendees of several different Baptist churches in Buncombe county, North Carolina, between the ages of 25 and 84. Three subgroups were produced between the ages of 25-45, 46-65, and 66-85, and focus groups were held with each subgroup. Although the entire group cited membership to the Baptist church, some members identified as regular churchgoers while others did not, normalizing the role of faith in the study's results. The study identified a common set of barriers shared across generations explaining the low advance directive completion rate in African Americans, along with a set of barriers that varied. Barriers in common included hesitancy about surrogate decision making, lack of education about advance care directive completion, and simple fear and denial about the need for advance directives. Only the younger focus group expressed ideas about spiritual acceptance of fatalities ("When it's time to go, it's time to go"), while only the middle-aged group expressed a mistrust of the healthcare system. Thus, mistrust for the US healthcare system seems to be a generationally localized trauma, whereas a reluctance to consider one's mortality appeared to persist throughout generations.

A different, more contemporary study trying to elucidate the role of parental trauma on the development of adolescent children chose a population group comprised purely of Cambodian high-school children whose parents had survived the Khmer Rouge genocide (Field, 2011). The large sample size of two hundred population ensured no demographic bias was represented in the results. Understanding Cambodian generational trauma is slightly tricky in that the entire country of Cambodia experienced some form of trauma from the Khmer Rouge massacre, and thus it is not feasible to produce a comparable untraumatized control group for a comparative study as has been done regularly when studying Holocaust survivor trauma (Barel, 2010). However, by excluding any data directly reported from the parents of the children, the study is somewhat biased towards the experiences of the children and relies on a limited understanding of the parents' unique traumas that may not be obvious to the children. This limitation is recognized by the study, which rightly suggests further studies apply more comprehensive population selection.

Conclusion

Generational trauma is a phenomenon that can present itself in the lives of future generations in the form of psychological, behavioural and emotional distress. The intensity of its manifestation can range from subtle emotional or psychological trauma to the development of serious mental disorders such as PTSD, depression, and anxiety. Although the children of holocaust survivors have been studied most extensively in this field, new research has focused on the children of historically oppressed populations such as Native

Americans and African Americans in the US, indigenous populations in Canada, as well as the children of refugees from war torn countries, and the children of survivors of other incidents of genocide such as in Rwanda and Cambodia. Using a holistic approach to study generational trauma allows us to understand the extent of its impact. Having a better understanding of its impact also allows us to produce better models for diagnosis of individuals with generational trauma, and to provide them with more effective treatment. Studying generational trauma from a psychological viewpoint is naturally the first method that comes to mind, however studying it from a sociological lens allows us to identify the behaviours in previous generations that may have led to transference of the trauma. Examining historically traumatized and oppressed communities can help us identify whether there are specific ways in which secondary trauma affects future generations, as well as helping us distinguish traumas that may simply be due to cultural or even local factors. Interviewing people regarding their personal experiences and how trauma has affected their lives can provide great insight into the impact and importance of studying generational trauma, however the results vary greatly between individuals and well as across entire communities. Each method of investigation therefore provides information regarding different aspects of generational trauma, and in order to fully understand this phenomenon it is essential to use a multi-faceted approach.

Chapter 5: What are Epigenetic Factors?
Yash Joshi

Introduction

Epigenetics refers to the field of study of how one's behaviour, actions, and external environment can impact their genes. It is further described as an area of study that investigates factors beyond an individual's deoxyribonucleic acid (DNA) sequence that impact genetic control (Simmons, 2008). Epigenetic changes can determine which genes are turned on and which proteins are transcribed from the existing DNA. Epigenetic silencing is one process through which gene expression is turned off. Within cells, there are three systems that can interact with each other to silence genes: DNA methylation, histone modification, and ribonucleic (RNA) associated silencing (Simmons, 2008). Epigenetic factors are then those specific parts within a cell, environment, or behaviours that lead to epigenetic changes. Although external epigenetic factors can be easily recognized such as smoking and environmental pollutants, those within the body are usually not acknowledged. In one's body, there are many molecules which impact epigenetics like various types of RNA such as messenger RNA (mRNA), long non-coding RNA (lncRNA), and micro RNA (miRNA). There are also proteins known as prions which have been known to have epigenetic effects. Collectively, these various molecules have a significant involvement in epigenetics through various functions.

The impact of mRNA

For a long time it was believed that it was not possible for chemical tags on genes to affect their expression without altering the DNA sequence itself. This belief has been challenged by discoveries surrounding mRNA and the field of epigenetics. mRNA is a molecule that behaves as the intermediate step between DNA translation and protein production by ribosomes in the cytoplasm of a cell (Pardi et al., 2018). They play an integral role as they carry information from DNA to ribosomes to eventually produce proteins, which would not be possible without them. Research has found that epigenetic markers are easily visible on mRNA molecules (Garber, 2019). RNA biologist Pedro Batista has said that cells use these markers to determine how much of the specific protein should be generated (Garber, 2019). The generation of proteins is necessary to ensure the proper function of the body. Furthermore, researcher Michael Kharas has shared that mRNA modifications can affect the viability of cells, cell division, cancer, and neurological diseases (Garber, 2019). While some of these modifications may be positive, many are negative and can increase mortality for an individual.

Modified mRNAs were initially reported in the 1970s but were not a major focus of research until 2008 (Garber, 2019). The renewed interest in modified mRNA emerged because of findings related to one specific modification. At this point, a group of researchers focused on one mRNA modification known as m6A, which is a methyl group attached to a few of an RNA molecule's adenine bases (Garber, 2019). The group noticed that a well-known enzyme, FTO or ALKBH5, was able to remove this mRNA modification, indicating that m6A played an important biological role because of the potential control over marked mRNA (Garber, 2019; Tian et al., 2021). m6A is the best-studied mRNA modification out of around half a dozen others. When proteins known as readers attach to m6A, they control the marked mRNA in various different ways (Garber, 2019). In blood stem cells, m6A restricts differentiation while in embryonic stem cells m6A boosts gene expression to properly differentiate into different cell types. Multiple studies in 2017 showed that eliminating the enzyme that adds m6A on mRNA kills tumour cells in acute myeloid leukemia (Garber, 2019). As a result, a few biotechnology companies have begun to work on experimental drugs to block such enzymes to eventually work towards treating cancers like leukemia.

The impact of lncRNAs

lncRNA is a specific type of RNA which is a certain size (longer than 200 nucleotides) and does not get translated into functional proteins, hence the 'non-coding' part of its name (Statello et al., 2021). They are a group of RNAs whose function is not fully understood. It can be seen that lncRNAs regulate gene expression in their own way because either the actual transcript is functional or because of the act of their transcription (Gibney & Nolan, 2010). Evidence of the functionality of lncRNAs is demonstrated through the fact that they have tissue-specificity, are regulated during development, localize to certain cellular areas, are associated with human disease, and/or portray clues of evolutionary selection (Wilusz et al., 2009). lncRNAs can also have regulatory effects. One specific interaction of lncRNAs is their involvement with chromatin-modifying enzymes (Gibney & Nolan, 2010). For example, HOTAIR, a lncRNA transcribed with the HOXC cluster, binds to the polycomb repressive complex PRC2 and targets the HOXD cluster to repress several genes (Rinn et al., 2007). A study by Khalil et al. (2009) showed that a considerable amount of lncRNAs in various human cell types are associated with complexes that add repressive chromatin marks and function in a target-specific manner. Thus, the unique patterns of lncRNAs in different cell types and their interactions with chromatin-altering complexes highlight a possible mechanism for creating and maintaining the epigenetic characteristics of certain cells.

Modifications on mRNA/lncRNA

lncRNA and mRNA in mammals contain tens of thousands of post-transcriptional chemical modifications, with m6A being the most abundant (N. Liu & Pan, 2015). m6A is present at three sites and also has the ability to be removed. Modification by the m6A molecule is recognized by families of RNA binding proteins that affect many aspects of mRNA function. This modification, as well as that by lncRNA, represents a layer of epigenetic regulation similar to DNA methylation and histone modification (N. Liu & Pan, 2015). Over 100 types of post-transcriptional changes have been noted in cellular RNA since the 1950s, as seen in human ribosomal RNA which itself has over 200 modifications consisting of three major types (N. Liu & Pan, 2015). Another type of modification is m5C which occurs internally in mRNA (N. Liu & Pan, 2015). These modifications share the characteristics that they cannot be detected by reverse transcriptase in cDNA synthesis, hence making them difficult to map as a single nucleotide resolution. As for the functions of m6A modification, some suggested impacts are on mRNA splicing, transport, stability, and immune tolerance (Bokar, 2005; Karikó et al., 2005). These functions play a significant role within the human body, highlighting the importance of the m6A molecule and its modifications. Interest in mRNA/lncRNA modifications resurfaced a few years ago when it was revealed that m6A modification is the cellular substrate for the human enzyme FTO, which is associated with obesity and diabetes (Jia et al., 2011; N. Liu & Pan, 2015). With the discovery of FTO acting on m6A, it became known that m6A modification is responsible for complex cellular control.

Furthermore, it is believed that RNA modification may act as an epigenetic marker and control similar to DNA methylation and histone modification. Three groups of proteins are needed for epigenetic control that maintains specific modification patterns at specific sites: writers, which catalyze chemical changes at sites, erasers, which remove modifications, and readers, to identify the modified sites in DNA or histones (N. Liu & Pan, 2015). All three groups of proteins have been found in mammalian cells for m6A in mRNA/lncRNA (N. Liu & Pan, 2015). It is widely believed that in the coming years, the number of reader proteins that recognize m6A modified mRNA/lncRNA will increase. Only the m6A modification currently has been shown to portray all the evidence of epigenetic regulation (N. Liu & Pan, 2015). Numerous different biological processes are affected through m6A modification and the modification has also been associated with a variety of human diseases. For example, m6A methyl transferases, specifically METTL3 and METTL14 play an integral role for cell development and their removal or depletion causes cell death (N. Liu & Pan, 2015). Furthermore, METTL3 has been associated with diseases such as prostatitis (the inflammation of the prostate gland) and aicardi syndrome, which is a rare,

X-linked genetic disorder which is mostly seen in females (N. Liu & Pan, 2015; Shah et al., 2009). Similarly, METTL14 has been linked to alcohol dependence (N. Liu & Pan, 2015). Most RNA methylations can be reversed by another enzyme in theory, although it has not been done so. Currently, m6A modification is the leading marker of RNA epigenetics.

The impact of microRNAs

MicroRNAs (miRNAs) are a group of non-protein coding RNAs which have been found to have potential for endogenous silencing. Endogenous silencing refers to the suppression of genes, hence why miRNAs have an integral role in gene regulation. Research has shown that miRNAs seem to be involved in numerous aspects of development, including the maintenance and establishment of tissue-specific expression profiles (Sætrom et al., 2007). Various non-protein coding RNAs are useful in altering the structure, sequence, or expression of mRNAs, and consequently the protein expression from these genes. For example, guide RNAs are used for RNA editing, small nuclear RNAs do gene splicing, telomere maintenance, transcription factor regulation, and small nucleolar RNA guides chemical changes to other RNA genes (Sætrom et al., 2007). There is not much information about miRNA regulation and transcription, but the best characterized miRNAs are a result of RNA polymerase II transcripts or introns or exons of protein-coding or nonprotein-coding genes (Sætrom et al., 2007). Additionally, mutations that result in new miRNAs in introns are believed to be an appropriate and effective mechanism to have well-regulated miRNA and drive animal evolution (Smalheiser & Torvik, 2005).
Cleavage is the strongest and most specific mechanism

between miRNA and mRNA and mRNA must produce a near ideal complex for cleavage to occur (Sætrom et al., 2007). Translation suppression and degradation both require less complementation between the base pairs of mRNA and miRNAs (Brennecke et al., 2005). These processes alter gene expression in different ways and highlight how miRNAs can affect an individual based on base pair complementation. A single miRNA has the capacity to regulate hundreds of genes, as seen in an experiment with miR-1 and miR-124 in which each miRNA down-regulated more than 100 mRNAs (Lim et al., 2005). With each miRNA having the potential to make such a drastic change, it is further showcased that these molecules can have significant impact in the field epigenetics. Some papers have described how miRNA expression is tissue-specific during development, which suggests that miRNAs are crucial to establishing and maintaining cell type and tissue identity (Sætrom et al., 2007). Not only that, over-expression of tissue-specific miRNAs has shown that a single miRNA has the ability to change the gene expression profile of an entire cell (Lim et al., 2005). Hence, just like lncRNAs and mRNAs, miRNAs are epigenetic factors that frequently have a role in modifying gene expression, just in their own way.

Other types of RNA

RNA-based mechanisms of epigenetic regulation are not as well understood as DNA methylation and histone based techniques (Gibney & Nolan, 2010). Other than lncRNAs, mRNAs, and miRNAs, there are specific forms of RNA that also play a role as epigenetic factors. For example, non-coding RNAs (ncRNAs) have been the subject of significant study and include a variety of types which are involved in translation and splicing and function by sequence-specific recognition of RNA substrates (Gibney & Nolan, 2010). Some of these ncRNAs have an additional regulatory role and are usually classified based on length, subcellular location, and orientation with respect to the nearest protein-coding gene (Gibney & Nolan, 2010). lncRNAs are a part of the broader category of ncRNAs, but there are other ncRNAs which have unique behaviours and impacts different than that of lncRNAs. Uniquely, ncRNAs, which are involved in chromatin remodelling, are believed to be involved in epigenetic inheritance (Manjrekar, 2017). The process exists as chromatin is a complex of DNA that contains histones which package DNA into a cell nucleus. Thus, changes to chromatin are bound to directly impact gene expression and lead to epigenetic inheritance. Additionally, there are also short-interfering RNAs (siRNAs) which usually base-pair with their target mRNAs and direct them to degradation, but sometimes repress translation if they base-pair with a less complementary target (Gibney & Nolan, 2010). They also take part in transcriptional gene silencing, which is highlighted in plants.

The impact of Prions

A prion is a protein which is improperly folded that triggers other normal proteins to fold abnormally (Centers for Disease Control and Prevention, 2018). Prions were initially discovered in mammals and regarded as infectious protein particles that were responsible for transmissible spongiform encephalopathies, which is a family of rare transmissible neurodegenerative brain disorders (Manjrekar, 2017). Prions were later also discovered in yeasts and fungi, further complicating their mode of transmission. . While prions, like other epigenetic modifications, may be inherited, prion-based inheritance occurs at the protein level rather than through indirect or direct modifications of gene expression (Manjrekar, 2017). This is different from DNA methylation and histone modification which involve the modification of gene expression. The frequency of prion formation is influenced by the presence of other prions and environmental conditions, like high temperature (Manjrekar, 2017). Prions are special because they cause the segregation of prion particles to daughter cells after cell division and make normally folded proteins into prions (Manjrekar, 2017). A process as such is not seen anywhere else and it helps prions transfer information between generations. Transformation into a prion typically results in loss of function for the protein, hence why the prion state creates protein shapes similar to those caused by loss-of-function mutations (Manjrekar, 2017). This overall is an efficient process, but not perfectly efficient, leading to rare prion loss at times.

Prions have the capacity to adopt at least one shape that self-templates over long biological periods (Harvey et al., 2018). As a result, they become protein-based epigenetic elements which persist in the body through mitosis and meiosis. Even though it was initially thought to be rare, protein-based epigenetic inheritance has now been discovered in all domains of life (Harvey et al., 2018). The complex folding of prion proteins allows them to move information across generations through the inheritance of stable, infectious protein conformations (Harvey et al., 2018). Prions usually contain Q/N-rich amino acid sequences that are organized in domains, which cause the production of prion strains. Within these domains, even small changes in sequence can lead to major problems in transmission between species.

Prion strains are one of the most unique epigenetic factors because they are distinct, transmissible epigenetic changes that are formed by one protein (Harvey et al., 2018). Different strains of prions differ structurally, in the size and stability of the formed aggregates, and in the stronger or weaker phenotypes produced (Manjrekar, 2017). In a way, prion strains are similar to allelic series of a gene. It has also been noted that epigenetic switching between prion and native states could increase flexibility for adaptation compared to genetic changes (Harvey et al., 2018). Genetic changes cannot easily revert back if environmental changes are no longer beneficial. Stability of prions through mitotic cell divisions varies greatly even though most methods of epigenetic inheritance allow for a large transmission of phenotypes (Harvey et al., 2018). DNA methylation and histone modification, the two most familiar methods of epigenetic inheritance, are relatively stable from dozens to tens of thousands of mitotic divisions (Harvey et al., 2018). Some recently discovered prion states have stability similar to that of histone modification, while a few others are typically as stable as DNA methylation. Thus, the overall heritability of prions differs greatly from other protein aggregates, which are usually retained in only mother cells (B. Liu et al., 2010; Zhou et al., 2014). Regardless of the stability, prions represent a unique epigenetic factor that allows researchers to explore disease and the human body in a new way.

Conclusion

There are a variety of epigenetic factors which greatly impact a person's life on a daily basis. Outside of external factors, there are many aspects within the body other than one's DNA sequence that can have a major influence on a person. mRNA is one of these, as some mRNA modifications have been shown to create effects like increased mortality, making it an area of study many companies and researchers are interested in. Interest in epigenetics has also brought focus onto lncRNA, which have a similar type of epigenetic regulation to that of DNA methylation and histone modification. Prions play a role as protein based epigenetic elements that have the capacity to transfer information across generations through infectious protein phenotypes. These various epigenetic factors have been of great interest to those in the epigenetic field for a while and will continue to be looked into to further understand epigenetics.

Chapter 7: What questions does the discovery of the link between events of history and generational trauma create?

Peter Anto Johnson

History and Generational Trauma

World history is a lineup of catastrophes creating generational trauma that arose from imperialism and colonialism. In the past, over two-thirds of the world's population was subject to European imperialism and its devastating consequences (Porter, 2016). These hegemonic, historical interactions between nations have left legacies that continue to wreak havoc in the contemporary era.
One such legacy was the Rwandan genocide of 1994 (Taylor, 2020). Most Europeans at that time, during the apex of social Darwinism, supported an ethnocentric worldview that perceived those of European origin as 'superior species' obligated to preside over other nations as a civilizing force (Shohat & Stam, 2014). When the Belgians colonized Rwanda, the home of the Hutu and Tutsi indigenous groups, they favored and elevated Tutsis to higher positions in society since they were more European-like and thus, genetically 'superior' to the Hutus (Taylor, 2020). When the Belgians left Rwanda, civil conflict erupted between the Hutus and Tutsis. Although peace agreements temporarily subdued the violence, the friction between the two tribes remained. On April 6, 1994, a plane carrying the Rwandan Hutu president,

Juvenal Habyarima, was shot down. The Hutus accused the Tutsis. Radio broadcasts gave Hutu civilians permission to take "revenge on the Tutsis." By July 19, 1994, over a million Rwandans were slaughtered. The UN Security Council attempted to create a Criminal Tribunal for Rwanda; however, prosecuting more than 130 000 people would take more than an estimated 200 years. To help out, local governments cooperated by instituting Rwandan gacaca courts – community courts to try those accused of low-level genocide crimes making the process of reconciliation about two times faster. This horrific event, like many others, perpetuated an

Theories on the Origins of Generational Trauma

Most of the conflict that has emerged and propagated generational trauma in the history of human civilization are a result of the walls people create between themselves. Dr. Paul Farmer's statement, "the idea that some lives matter less is the root of all that's wrong with the world," reflects one result this division creates, a distorted mentality based on principles of inequality (Farmer, 2004). The divergence this division creates between individuals spark conflict within and between societies. In nature, speciation forms distinct biological species over time because of geographical, behavioral, physiological or other biological barriers. In one case in Central America, a species of shrimps were isolated by geographical barriers and after having diverged into separate species were placed together (Munoz et al., 2009). These two species, as members of the same species, had courted peacefully. After becoming two discrete species however, they demonstrated violent aggression towards one other. The same can be assumed about human aggression and conflict as similar principles apply to humans. If the conception of this barrier were extended, the seclusion of two sets of subjects regardless of population size would cause each set to undergo subtle or immense change due to any range of variables. After a significant duration, if this barrier was lifted and the subjects could interact, there is a higher prospect for conflict than in their initial interaction. Protracting this analogy, global conflict is founded on walls that distance people through affiliations like nations over generations. Conflicts, consequences of a long period of division, tend to originate from inadvertence, contrary views, and environmental factors.

Over the course of time, generational trauma can manifest as separate groups advancing distinct ideologies, cultural values, and beliefs, which could be inconsistent with the standpoint of others. One such occasion when views collided was during the period of the Cold War between 1945 and 1991 (Gaddis, 2006; Whitfield, 1996). The US headed the Western world and the Soviet Union dominated the Eastern world. Since both nations possessed nuclear weapons capable of a nuclear holocaust, most of the conflicts between the nations were proxy wars within other regions between groups indoctrinated with the Soviet Union's ideology of socialism and collectives following the liberal democracy ideology of the US. One significant event was the establishment of the Berlin Wall drawing a line between East and West Berlin (Major, 2010). The creation of this border demonstrates the Soviet Union's desire to reaffirm walls that existed before the conflict. The elimination of the geographical and psychological barrier resulted in an ideological war. The overlapping of political dogmas led the conflict, the means to proclaim one correct ideology.

Most importantly, the desire for power and equality initiates conflict. Imperialism from the late nineteenth century to early twentieth century has influenced several nations within the world (Porter, 2016). Returning to the example of the Rwandan genocide, the conquests for the expansion of colonies and power led German and Belgian imperialism to plant the seeds for bloody conflicts within the nation of Rwanda (Taylor, 2020). Sprouting from supremacist approaches that deny the worth of other cultures, the German and Belgian invaders established a hierarchy in Rwanda based on biological similarities. Crowning the European culture as the supreme species above all else, the pyramid focused Tutsis, a minority ethnic group within Rwanda with inherent physical features resembling stereotypical Europeans, directly below them. At the lowest level sat the Hutus, the group with the fewest physiological similarities. Until Rwanda gained independence from the imperial powers in 1962, the Hutus were socially excluded, given few privileges, and treated harshly. Without the weight of the imperial powers in the pyramid, the Hutus scrambled from under the pyramid in a revolt against the Tutsis. The Rwandan civil war from 1990 to 1993 between the Hutus and Tutsis ended the aristocracy and temporarily created a society with equality. In 1994, the assassination of the presiding Hutu representative government, Juvenal Habyarimana, ignited the genocide of billions of Tutsis. The geographical, psychological and biological wall that separated the imperialists, the Tutsis and Hutus were undeniably the underlying cause of this mass massacre. Generally, conflict arises from inequality and the emotions for an aspect within the other society.

Though conditional, conflict arises from the differences a dividing wall creates over time. The development of global peace therefore depends on both, the elimination of these fences creating apartheid and the redefinition of where the walls of the universe end. The solution lies in the creation of permanent cooperative networks that all members of the world can be part of and at the same time reach an agreement on (Gareis, 2012). The United Nations are the closest modern model to this network and the accommodation of many voices in the world. Although some solutions require the establishment of barriers, these barriers should be semi-permeable based on moral principles, according to the beliefs of individuals yet still open to the rest of the world. Global acceptance and principles of accommodation are vital for the development of a world without conflict.

Legacies of Generational Trauma in Canada

In Canada, one of the major driving forces for the mistrust in our social, educational, and healthcare system is the mistreatment of Aboriginal people. Indigenous peoples, composed of First Nations (Indian), Inuit, and Métis make up just under 5% of the national Canadian population, yet remain marginalized and underrepresented in many facets of civil life (Gordon, 2006).

In the late 18th century, the early settlers gradually became the mainstream culture of Canada and eventually set up governance over Canada (Francis, 1998), eventually pushing Indigenous folk to the periphery - both in a literal sense geographically and in a figurative sense. The Canadian government started implementing policies of assimilation of Aboriginal culture into the more European "Canadian culture" which borrowed ideals of Christianity, sedentary living, autonomy, education, and freedom.

Under the Indian Act of 1876 came the creation of Indian reserves, which were subject to restrictive laws such bans on all intoxicants, restrictions on eligibility to vote, decreased hunting and fishing areas, and inability for status Indians to visit other groups on their reservations (Francis, 1998). These historical moves are important to consider because they still affect inidgenous folks today, who are displaced or otherwise alienated from their clans. The estrangement of indigineous groups from their families and tribes caused the oral traditions of storytelling and cosmology to be lost in exchange for more Western ideas around science and empirical knowledge.

The final government strategy of assimilation was the Canadian residential school system (1847 – 1996) – a system of 130 boarding schools nation-wide, designed to lead children most effectively out of their niches and systematically indoctrinate them to walk, talk, and behave like their European counterparts (Grant, 1996; Lavallee & Poole, 2010). This form of assimilation essentially wiped out a vast majority of the cosmological and astrological history that was shared by parents to children often orally. Since the narratives shared from parent to child were often not written, these stories became effectively erased and replaced by classical liberal and more "Western" ideals.

These schools were underfunded and plagued by death and disease (e.g. TB) alongside physical, emotional, and sexual abuse (Lavallee & Poole, 2010). Children were prohibited from speaking their native tongue or carrying out their cultural traditions and customs. The residential school experience in Canada meets the UN criteria for genocide. A legal case resulted in a settlement of $2 billion in 2016 and the establishment of the Truth and Reconciliation Commission (TRC) which confirmed the detrimental effect on children and all Aboriginal Canadians and looks to remedy the lasting effects of the historic mistreatment. The TRC continues to be one of the leading bodies in Canada trying to enact justice for Aboriginal populations in Canada and similar groups exist in other North American countries to attempt similar feats.

Although the health of Aboriginal populations in Canada has been improving in recent years, significant health disparities exist between Aboriginal/non-Aboriginal Canadians due to generational trauma (Lavallee & Poole, 2010). Virtually every health indicator and social determinant of health suggests that the health of Indigenous peoples in Canada is significantly poorer than that of the remainder population. For example, smoking/drinking rates, obesity rates, education, income, SES, employment rates, access to healthcare, overcrowding and poor housing conditions, life expectancy, birth rates, mortality rates are all associated with Aboriginal peoples (Lavallee & Poole, 2010).

Legacies of Generational Trauma for the Basques

Another contemporary example of the legacies of generational trauma are evident in the population of Basques displaced and living in parts of Spain and France. The Basques are considered a nation as they share a common culture, history, language, geography, ethnicity and spirituality (Allieres, 2016; Aguirre et al., 1991). In their understanding, nationhood is ultimately defined by tradition. For example, land was viewed as a symbol of the nation's ancestral history. This was because the inheritance of land was deeply embedded in Basque tradition. Similarly, the Basque language served as another persevering icon of their national identity. Despite the assimilating pressures of surrounding nation-states, the Basque language has continued to thrive. Like many European states, the Basque people adopted Roman Catholicism; however after the Spanish and Portuguese Inquisitions, refugees introduced Judaism and Islam to Basque. Even though the traditional Basque country became part of France and Spain, some Basques still fight for separationist values as others became assimilated into mainstream society.

These people were stolen of their political sovereignty. Like many indigenous cultures, Basques followed egalitarian forms of government until the influence of neighboring states feudalized Basque society (Allieres, 2016). During the 1500s, the Basques became victims of the Spanish civil war which raged on for nine years. Although the majority of Basque land laid in ruins, the Basques were fortunate to self-govern themselves, but the advent of the French Revolution followed by successive civil wars put an abrupt end to their self-government. During this time, many Basques were displaced from their traditional land as they fled to the West. The Basques could not make a fast recovery as many European countries at the time embraced expansionist attitudes for the sake of national prestige.

Basques people still do not have the freedom to self-govern themselves. Many are required to participate as members of surrounding nation-states (Allieres, 2016). The Basque region is separated into administrative units but they do not have official status to be part of other countries' politics. Even with minor political support, there are a large number of Basque nationalists that wage campaigns and demonstrate advocating for a separate Basque nation. Even in the past, the Spanish crown offered the Basques little opportunity to separate and simply tweaked with legislations to ease the absorption of the Basques into the prevalent cultural dominion (Molina, 2010). In many cases, the French and Spanish administrations have turned a blind eye to issues affecting the Basques. Little progress has been made as it is evident that they are being repressed even in present-day Spain and France and that generational trauma still persist in these populations.

Chapter 8: Why is it important to study Epigenetics?

Nazihah Alam

Introduction to Importance of Studying Epigenetics

Epigenetics modification is the changing of the function of a cell, which is through changing the instructions of the cell in the genome, without changing the actual DNA sequence. There are different types of epigenetic changes, as mentioned in earlier chapters, such as DNA methylation, histone modification, and non-coding RNA (U.S. National Library of Medicine, 2020). Depending on the specific epigenetic change, some could remain permanent while others may reverse over time due to the environmental conditions present at that time (Centers for Disease Control and Prevention, 2020). Epigenetic changes can affect an individual's health in both positive and negative manners. This is why it is important to study epigenetics, to be more informed on how it could be useful in today's society. This chapter will focus on the relationship epigenetics has with cancer, diabetes and addiction. It will take a closer look at what genomic imprinting is and the importance of public health's attention on the matter.

Epigenetics and Cancer

An individual is made up of over a billion cells which are continuously growing, dividing through cell division, and then dying when they are old or damaged (National Cancer Institute, 2021). However, there are situations where a damaged cell divides uncontrollably or the old cell does not die off like normal, which can lead to an excessive amount of cells that can form a tumor (National Cancer Institute, 2021). There are two categories of tumors, they can either be cancerous, also known as malignant, or non cancerous, which is also known as benign. Malignant tumors can spread to nearby tissues and form more tumors in the process, this is known as metastasis (American Cancer Society, 2020). Benign tumors on the other hand do not spread, but they can grow in size, which can become life threatening (National Cancer Institute, 2021).

There are several types of cancer, a few of the most common types of cancer are breast cancer, lung cancer and colon and rectum cancer (World Health Organization, 2021). There can be many factors causing cancer, it is often an interplay between genetic and environmental factors. Epigenetic mechanisms can be used as a treatment of cancer because of its reversible possibility and flexibility. Using epigenetic measures to interfere with the formation of tumors and suppress tumor growth is a complicated process that can take a combination of therapies (Cheng et al., 2019). At the same time, it is important to note that certain types of cancers might arise from epigenetic changes, thus having more trials and research is essential in figuring out what epigenetic changes can help or lead to cancer (Cheng et al., 2019). There are many clinical experiments that are looking at different combinations of epigenetic drugs and immunotherapy methods (Cheng et al., 2019).

Epigenetics and Diabetes

Diabetes is a disease where an individual's body is either unable to produce its own or it cannot use its own insulin. Insulin plays an important function in the body because it helps control the amount of glucose in the blood. Insulin is a hormone which is developed in the pancreas (Sharma et al., 2020).There are three types of diabetes, Type 1 diabetes, type 2 diabetes and gestational diabetes. In type 1 diabetes, an individual is unable to produce insulin to suffice the body. In type 2 diabetes the body is able to create insulin, however it is not used effectively leading to concerns. Gestational diabetes occurs in women who are pregnant, but it can go away once the baby is delivered. Another important stage of diabetes, called prediabetes, where individuals are experiencing symptoms that are showing a higher chance of diabetes. It is best to tackle the issue at the prediabetes stage before it is diagnosed as diabetes (Mayo Foundation for Medical Education and Research, 2020). Diabetes is considered to be a lifestyle disease, where certain behaviour changes can prevent diabetes even after getting prediabetic symptoms. If diabetes is not maintained, it can lead to other serious health concerns such as cardiovascular disease or obesity. There remains a large study opportunity to learn about the exact mechanisms that cause diabetes (Sharma et al., 2020)

There is a growing number of evidence where epigenetics can play an important role in helping diabetes. Epigenetics could become a bridgeway between the gene and environmental factor relationship, which are both crucial in diabetes (Sharma et al., 2020). Glucose levels can affect several tissues in the body such as adipose tissue, liver and skeletal muscle. Recent studies have also shown that the microbiome in the intestines have an association with type 1 diabetes and type 2 diabetes. Murri and her colleagues did a case control study that looked at the differences of gut microbiota between children who had type 1 diabetes and children who were deemed healthy. The study results showed an association between the microbiomes in the gut and type 1 diabetes (Murri et al., 2013). Children with type 1 diabetes intestinal structure and function was deemed poorer than the intestines of healthy children, which indicates the possibility of finding ways to improve the intestinal conditions in children with type one diabetes could be beneficial, hence the role of epigenetics (Murri et al., 2013). In the case of type two diabetes, certain epigenetic processes, DNA methylation can affect insulin resistance in human bodies by targeting the pancreatic islets (Sharma et al., 2020).

Genomic imprinting

A human being receives genes from both paternal and maternal sides, however according to genomic imprinting, only one side of a copy is expressed in the offspring (Lobo, 2008). This is done through the process of DNA methylation, where the expressed allele is unmethylated and the expressed allele is methylated (Bajrami & Spiroski, 2016). An allele is one part in the pair of genes, an offspring will receive one pair per specified characteristic. Depending on where those genes are located on the specific chromosome, it can determine different physical characteristics of a person. Alleles become phenotypes which produce eye colour, hair colour or blood type. There are both dominant alleles and recessive alleles, dominant alleles are always expressed when paired with a recessive allele which is masked. Recessive alleles are only expressed if both copies are recessive in the pairs (The Public Engagement team at the Wellcome Genome Campus, 2016).

Genomic imprinting can lead to various health concerns and causes of diseases because of the modifications. One of those diseases is Prader Willi Syndrome which was officially reported in 1956 by Andrea Prader, Alexis Labhart and Heinrich Willi (Bajrami & Spiroski, 2016). Prader-Willi syndrome affects both cognitive and behavioural functions (Bajrami & Spiroski, 2016). Most of the cases are seen to be caused by a small portion on chromosome 15 being deleted from the paternal copy (U.S. National Library of Medicine, 2020). During this time the maternal copy is not being expressed. In the 25% of people with Prader-Willi syndrome it occurs because instead of receiving a copy from each parent, both copies are from the maternal side (U.S. National Library of Medicine, 2020). This process is known as maternal uniparental disomy, where only the maternal side is expressed. Another health concern that can arise from genomic imprinting is Angleman syndrome, founded in 1965 by Harry Angleman (Bajrami & Spiroski, 2016). Angelman Syndrome is also caused by problems on chromosome 15 (Mayo Foundation for Medical Education and Research., 2020). In this case it can be due to the maternal copy having a small portion which is either deleted or has been damaged. In fewer cases, it can be due to the inheitment of two paternal copies rather than the normal (Mayo Foundation for Medical Education and Research, 2020). Genomic imprinting can also lead to various types of cancers because it can lead to unintentional mass cell growth which can cause a tumor (Bajrami & Spiroski, 2016).

Addiction's Effect on Epigenetic Changes

Addiction is when the brain or body wants a particular substance or behaviour without considering the possible repercussions of the action (Tyler, 2018). They may lack a sense of self-control due to the obsession (Tyler, 2018). Addiction can hinder a person's lifestyle, from the relationships around them to their health or to their financial situation (Tyler, 2018). They may also fall in cycles, where there are periods of remission where the person is able to abstain from the addiction, but depending on the person there can also be relapse where the person falls back into habit and sometimes it is even worse than before (Tyler, 2018). It is a serious concern and it is encouraged to seek treatment as soon as possible. There are many different methods to treat addiction, thus an individual can look for what works for them best and try it out. The environmental conditions can influence epigenetic changes made in the body. In particular, it can change the structure of the DNA at a multitude of levels, which can in turn lead to certain health outcomes and inheritable traits (National Institute on Drug Abuse, 2019). An example of this is when an individual uses cocaine, it can affect the development of protein in the system. Histones, which are part of the family of proteins, are used as the base where DNA coils around it. Depending on how tight or loose those strands are, it can change how the gene is expressed. Genes are the units that make up DNA strands. Certain substances can affect the coiling of the histones leading to modifications on the gene expression

(National Institute on Drug Abuse, 2019). Knowing this information can be beneficial in the future, as scientists and researchers can look further into how the coiling can help change the gene expressions of different disorders (National Institute on Drug Abuse, 2019).

Public Health and the Field of Epigenetics

The growing epigenetics field can become a topic for public health to look at. Through clinical and epidemiological studies, it has been determined that epigenetics can occur due to both environmental and genetic factors (Melén et al., 2018). There are also implications of heritability of thes3333e changes, which would mean future generations could be affected, whether that be positively or negatively. There has been ongoing research on epigenetic changes and respiratory diseases (Melén et al., 2018). A recent genome-wide study on methylation has shown that DNA methylation and air pollution may have a relationship which can cause asthma or chronic obstructive pulmonary disease (Melén et al., 2018). Thus there are many aspects of epigenetics that align with other public health concerns, such as smoking and diabetes (Melén et al., 2018). The field of public health focuses on the health of the general population. Epigenetics has aspects that are similar to diabetes and smoking, in the fact that firstly it can be inheritable. The epigenetic changes made can be passed down through generations and affect both youth and adult populations (Melén et al., 2018). Second, the epigenetic changes can be flexible and reversible depending on the action taken (Melén et al., 2018). Third, epigenetics and the environment seem to play hand in hand, which would mean certain preventative measures could be taken to ensure there is lower risk of certain health concerns (Melén et al., 2018). Thus, this rising topic would be important for public health to take into consideration in the upcoming years.

Final Words

In conclusion, although the "epigenesis" concept was founded in the seventeenth century, the 21st century showed the greatest surgence of knowledge in the field. From this chapter, it has been noted how studying epigenetics can bring forward knowledge within various health concerns, such as cancer, diabetes and addiction. It also is used for studying genomic imprinting and learning about certain diseases within that realm, including Prader Willi Syndrome and Angelman Syndrome. Epigenetics plays a role in cell differentiation and genetic regulation. There is also ongoing research and experimentation for epigenetic drugs and therapy methods that can be useful against cancer. It is also important for public health figures to monitor the field of epigenetics as many aspects resemble other current public health concerns. As it can be seen, epigenetics not only focuses on individuals but it can touch many members of different populations, thus it is important to invest more time and funds to complete further clinical studies and research.

Chapter 9: Does Generational Trauma Really Exist?

Yash Joshi

Introduction

The idea of generational trauma has been a topic of discussion amongst experts ever since its discovery in 1966. Generational trauma, also known as trans- or intergenerational trauma, is a concept that agrees that extreme events that impact individuals can be so severe that the consequences are also dealt by their offspring in the future (Yehuda & Lehrner, 2018).The term was coined initially in 1966 by a Canadian psychiatrist named Vivian M. Rakoff and her team who used the concept of generational trauma to explain high rates of psychological distress in children of holocaust survivors (Gillespie, 2020). Since then, there have been many discoveries and advancements in the field. Some studies further explored the idea of generational trauma and how applicable it would be to other people and situations. Many however questioned whether or not passing traumatic events from one generation to the next is actually possible, especially due to the biological implications. This has led to a great debate amongst experts in the field.

Studies on Generational Trauma

When the discovery related to the children of holocaust survivors was revealed, it led to great excitement regarding the concept of generational trauma. There were also other studies to further understand the concept, such as when scientists reported that children who were exposed in the womb to the Dutch Hunger Winter had a specific chemical mark, known as an epigenetic signature, on their genes (Carey, 2018). With an increasing amount of evidence, many researchers were beginning to believe that an individual inherits some aspect of their parents' and grandparents' trauma which affects that individuals' present life (Carey, 2018). These effects would possibly be carried forward into the certain individuals' offspring as well. Studies in mice have presented experimental evidence of trauma transmission, although the effects are small yet consistent.

While generational trauma has been an idea that many researchers are not fully convinced about, there have been studies conducted to prove that generational trauma exists. In a study by Perroud et al. the Tutsi genocide was studied, specifically the impact on the children of the women who were pregnant during the genocide (Perroud et al., 2014). They concluded that both mothers and their children who were exposed to the genocide had higher levels of post traumatic stress disorder (PTSD) and depression in comparison to the control group (Perroud et al., 2014). DNA methylation changes in exposed changes and their children were also highlighted, suggesting that trauma-induced methylation changes in humans can be transmitted from parents to children. There were limitations to the study due to the small sample size as well as possible confounding because both groups lived in different countries, the exposed group was not matched with the control group, and other factors such as health of participants at the time of study were also not acknowledged (Youssef et al., 2018).

In another study, Yehuda et al. (2016) looked into intergenerational methylation changes of Holocaust survivors on FKBP5, which behaves as a moderator of glucocorticoid activity. It was noted that the Holocaust survivors had higher FKBP5 intron 7 methylation levels, whereas their offspring had significantly lower levels (Yehuda et al., 2016). The authors suggested that the opposite effect seen might be related to biological accommodation in the offspring. Some limitations of the study included small sample size and the presence of other factors which are impossible to control, such as extreme starvation in Holocaust survivors. If the study was replicated on a larger scale, it may be able to provide significant information related to the generational inheritance of trauma and PTSD.

Other stresses have also been looked into as a study by Mulligan et al. (2012) investigated if prenatal maternal stress in the Congo population led to glucocorticoid receptor changes in offspring. Glucocorticoids are stress hormones (Youssef et al., 2018). These changes in offspring would increase the risk of adult-onset disease. The research group found that in 25 mother-newborn dyads, there was a significant correlation between stress in mothers and increased methylation levels on the promoter of the glucocorticoid receptor gene in newborns (Mulligan et al., 2012). The team suggested that the increased methylation in offspring might restrict plasticity in gene expression and reduce the range of stress adaptation responses, consequently increasing the risk of chronic disease in the future (Mulligan et al., 2012).

In a similar study, mothers who experienced pre-pregnancy or during pregnancy exposure to intimate partner violence and their children at the age of 10-19 were analyzed (Radtke et al., 2011). This was the first study to actually analyze the long term impacts of trauma on offspring (Youssef et al., 2018). The researchers found that the mother's experience of intimate partner violence during pregnancy affected the methylation of the NR3C1 promoter gene of the children (Radtke et al., 2011). It was believed that these modifications were done in the womb and may represent a possible mechanism through which prenatal stress can impact adult psychosocial function in offspring. The problem with these studies however is that they have a small sample size and often do not address other factors which can lead to the developmental of behaviours in offspring. Additionally, none of these studies specifically explain the biological mechanisms of how exactly the trauma is passed from an individual to subsequent offspring. It is worth noting that in numerous studies, the glucocorticoid receptor (NR3C1) gene is associated with methylation changes (Youssef et al., 2018). Further investigation into the glucocorticoid receptor gene may be beneficial in understanding the transmission of generational trauma.

The Issues with Generational Trauma

As for critics, many say that the biology behind the concept is not possible, specifically based on what is known so far in the fields of biology and genetics. The mechanism of intergenerational transmission of trauma is not understood. One possibility is that the transmission is based on social mechanisms, another is it is mediated by genetic or epigenetic changes (Cai et al., 2020). What has profound researchers is that no one is able to precisely explain how changes in brain cells caused by traumatic events can be transmitted to fully formed egg or sperm cells before conception (Carey, 2018). Additionally, after sperm and egg meet, a natural cleansing process occurs which strips away most chemical marks on the genes which complicates the theorized transmission process. Lastly, as the fertilized egg develops and grows, genetic reshuffling happens where cells begin to specialize, so it is unclear how the signature of trauma could still survive after that.

There have been experiments and ongoing studies to find answers to these questions and to validate the concept of generational trauma. In one study, mice were subject to difficult environments (periodical tilting of cages, leaving lights on at night) during their upbringing (Rodgers et al., 2013). These stimulated environments of a traumatic childhood changed the behaviour of these mice's genes in a way that affected their stress hormones. The consequences were also seen in the offspring as the young mice were numb and less reactive to the stress hormones, compared to the control mice in the study (Rodgers et al., 2013). Another explanation for the passing on of trauma is related to the marking of sperm before fertilization. In a study on mammalian sperm, it was seen that sperm cells in father's seemed to get marked in the epididymis, which is a tube near the testicles where sperm is stored and learns how to swim (Sharma et al., 2018). The team believes that the tube produces small ribonucleic acid (small RNA) and transports them to the sperm as the sperm develops (Sharma et al., 2018). That would then suggest that there is an area within the father's body where the RNA can be altered to pass on the trauma marks to the offspring. Although these are valid explanations, many critics of the theory still believe that there is not enough evidence to confidently say that this is how trauma is passed on between generations. Furthermore, these convincing results have only been shown in animal experiments. With human experiments, the results are not persuasive and a mechanism for epigenetic transmissions of trauma has not been shown (Carey, 2018). It is expected that experiments will continue to happen to discover a plausible mechanism to explain generational trauma, but until then many researchers will remain skeptical.

Understanding the Science of Generational Trauma

Understand some of the biology behind why transmitting trauma is difficult, one needs to analyze the human body. All somatic cells in a multicellular organism have the same genome but different cell types that have different transcriptomes (set of all expressed RNA molecules), different proteomes (set of all proteins), and consequently different functions (Horsthemke, 2018). Not only that, cell differentiation requires the repression and activation of certain genes. It is difficult to explain how the trauma marks would not get suppressed at this stage of cell differentiation. Further, germ cells are the cells which eventually give rise to gametes, also known as an organism's reproductive cells (Wylie & Anderson, 2002). For traits to be transmitted from one generation to the next, the epigenetic changes would also have to manifest in germ cells as well. While this has been known to occur, the specific changes for generational trauma have not been seen.

Other than genes, people also inherit from environments and culture, such as one's mother's womb. This environment can drastically impact health, as factors such as severe undernourishment can affect not only the pregnant woman, but their unborn offspring as well (Horsthemke, 2018). Genes and the environment affect the epigenome and the phenotype of an individual (Danchin et al., 2011). While culture affects the phenotype, there is not enough evidence to determine what impacts it has on the epigenome. Parents and offspring might share the same epigenomic features, but it is usually difficult to determine whether these features have been transmitted through germline or created newly in each generation due to shared genes and environments (Horsthemke, 2018). This information further reiterates why passing trauma from an individual to their offspring is not easy, because each individual even if they belong to the same family.

As for proving transgenerational epigenetic inheritance, certain tasks need to be done. Firstly, one must be able to rule out genetic, ecological, and cultural inheritance (Horsthemke, 2018). Although it is difficult to rule out ecological and cultural inheritance in human experiments, genetic impacts should be excluded. These circumstances are more easily produced with laboratory experiments. The next step would be actually identifying the epigenetic factor responsible for the changes within the germ cells (Horsthemke, 2018). This is difficult to do as female germ cells are scarce or unavailable and because germ cell preparation might come contaminated. For accurate results, the presence of somatic cells and somatic DNA must be excluded. Lastly, one needs to be able to show that the epigenetic factor in the germ cells is responsible for the phenotypic change in the following generation (Horsthemke, 2018). One way that this method can occur is removing the affected germ cells from a generation and then showing that the effect is lost, while adding the factor to controls will add the effect. The issue is that most of the required experiments cannot be done on humans. Generational inheritance of chromatin marks is rare in humans, and at times can be attributed to extensive epigenetic reprogramming needed for cell development and early embryosis (Horsthemke, 2018). Also, the transfer of epigenetic information between generations decreases developmental plasticity and narrows offspring into a certain type (Horsthemke, 2018). A decrease of diversity would occur as multiple offsprings would share the same information. Proving these methods in a laboratory might bring larger advancements to the field and potentially help solidify the case for generational trauma.

Possible mechanisms for Generational Trauma

Long-lived RNA molecules are less affected by barriers and are more likely to transfer epigenetic information across generations (Chen et al., 2016). These molecules have garnered interest from experts in the field as they may present a plausible mechanism to transfer trauma marks, but have yet to be thoroughly investigated. On the other hand, another possible mechanism to transfer trauma between generations that has been investigated is mitochondrial DNA (mtDNA). mtDNA is a small circular chromosome found inside mitochondria and there are hundreds to thousands of those in a single cell (Cai et al., 2020). Increased mtDNA values have been linked to psychological stress, hence why changes to mitochondrial function are investigated as mechanisms in stress-related conditions (Cai et al., 2020). Specific mtDNA studies have been done on Holocaust survivors. The Holocaust was a horrifying period and those who survived continued to deal with trauma related to the murdering of their friends, family, and community. In a study by Cai et al. (2020) mtDNA copy number in peripheral blood mononuclear cells from Holocaust survivors was compared to those without Holocaust experience. The team assumed that the mtDNA levels would have increased in Holocaust survivors as it was impossible to measure the values immediately after the Holocaust. They wanted to see if this number stayed elevated after a few decades and whether or not it can be inherited by their ancestors.

The researchers found no significant difference in the mtDNA copy number in Holocaust survivors companered to the controls (Cai et al., 2020). The lack of difference between the experimental and control group might be because mtDNA copy number may have reversed with time (Cai et al., 2015). The removal of stressful stimuli may be able to lead to the complete recovery of elevation in mtDNA copy number, hence why it would not be observed decades later (Cai et al., 2020). Another possibility is that Holocaust survivors are made up of resilient individuals, where their genetic factors might contribututte to the recovery of increased mtDNA copy number. The study also found lower mtDNA copy numbers in the children of Holocaust survivors (Cai et al., 2020). These results might be a consequence of other biological and environmental factors specific to descendants of Holocaust survivors.

The effect of parental Holocaust experiecne was not reported, meaning that its effect on mtDNA levels cannot be dismissed. The researchers observed higher levels of PTSD in the children of Holocaust survivors compared to the control cohort. This pattern was not seen in the grandchildren of Holocaust survivors, suggesting single generation inheritance of specific risk factors for PTSD. There is no evidence that mtDNA copy number elevation is one of these factors. Overall, the study was unable to find conclusive evidence of consistent mtDNA copy number changes in Holocaust survivors, and that mtDNA cannot be used to explain the inheritance of risk of PTSD in their descendants (Cai et al., 2020). Examining mtDNA and the inconclusive results are a representation of what researchers have been dealing with while attempting to prove generational trauma.

Conclusion

Overall, it can be noted that generational trauma is a concept that has been under discussion ever since its discovery in the 1960s. Starting with the initial study, many subsequent studies and researchers have found that at times trauma seems to be passed from an individual to their offspring. Whether it be Holocaust survivors or pregnant mother who face stressful environments, the trauma is passed on to their children in some form. It is unclear how the trauma is precisely passed on to the offspring because of the biology of trauma marks. Processes such as cell differentiation and the development of embryos make it difficult for genetic marks to still be present, hence complicating the passing of trauma. Studies have been done on possible mechanisms such as mtDNA, yet most have not succeeded in convincingly proving that generational trauma exists. This field does have the attention of many and will continue to develop in the future as researchers continue to look for ways to prove how trauma is passed from person to person.

Chapter 10: How are epigenetic theories used in practice?

Alyssa Wu

Introduction

The study of genetics involves understanding and investigating heritable changes in gene activity that result in the effects of direct alterations of the DNA sequence. Examples of genetic alterations include point mutations, deletions, insertions, and translocation (Moore et al., 2013). Epigenetics falls under a specific branch of genetics, a unique field of study that is focused on learning about the heritable and reversible forms of gene regulation that are not dependent on DNA sequencing (Heerboth et al., 2014). There are many types of epigenetic changes, including DNA methylation, histone methylation, acetylation, ubiquitination, and phosphorylation. The function of these epigenetic changes is to modify and alter gene expression within an organism. This is done at the level of transcription through upregulating, downregulating, or silencing genes that may not be used to create a functional protein or enzyme (Heerboth et al., 2014).

Therapeutic Interventions

There are a variety of drugs that inhibit the function of certain enzymes which can be used in epigenetic therapy. Some of the drugs that will be discussed in this chapter include DNA methylation inhibiting drugs, and bromodomain inhibitors. There are many functional similarities between these drugs as they all target a specific functional enzyme that can be helpful in controlling gene regulation within a cell.

DNA methylation inhibiting drugs are one of the oldest forms of methylation inhibitors (Heerboth et al., 2014). They are described as nucleoside-like compounds, which recruit proteins that are involved in the binding of various transcription factors to the DNA. Over time, as the cells grow and proliferate, differentiated cells will produce a stable and unique DNA methylation pattern that regulates tissue-specific gene transcription (Moore et al., 2013). DNA methylation is commonly used in cancer therapy, as many of these nucleoside compounds have been approved by the U.S. Food and Drug Administration (FDA) for the treatment of certain cancers (Heerboth et al., 2014). Some functions of DNA methylation used in clinical practice include silencing retroviral elements, regulating tissue-specific gene expression, genomic imprinting, and X chromosome inactivation. Previous research has shown that when DNA methylation is used in different genomic regions, it may influence other areas of gene activity based on the underlying genetic sequence (Moore et al., 2013).

Bromodomain inhibitors are defined as conserved structural motifs that are associated with chromatin-modifying proteins. There are currently 61 known types of bromodomains, one of the most common being histone acetyltransferases

(HATs) (Heerboth et al., 2014). Bromodomain inhibitors are considered to be "epigenetic reader domains and are the only protein structure known to recognize acetylated lysine residues" (Heerboth et al., 2014). HATs inhibit the catalytic activity that is a common clinical factor seen in many cancers and health diseases. However, HATs are not very chemically selective compounds, as they bind multiple classes of proteins (Heerboth et al., 2014). Therefore, using HATs alone in clinical practice is difficult because it is hard to control for which genes are being altered in the genetic sequence. This can result in adverse effects with unintended genetic modifications. Histone deacetylase inhibitors remove any existing acetylation found on histones. This makes DNA packaging more compact and tightly regulated to restrict access to transcription. Deacetylase inhibitors work cooperatively with histone-modifying enzymes to impose a repressive state on a gene region (Moore et al., 2013).

Protein methyltransferase (PMT) inhibitors have enzymatic activities that have potential pathological roles in cancer, neurodegenerative diseases, and inflammatory diseases (Heerboth et al., 2014). Targeted genetic studies have shown that the inhibition of PMTs functions to stop or pause these enzymatic alterations to control the rate of disease spread (Heerboth et al., 2014). Histone methylation inhibitors are newly classified inhibitors that were synthesized to prevent trimethylation. This was done because developmentally regulated genes were found to be reactivated through the process of trimethylation. As these developmental genes are not always silenced by DNA methylation, these histone methylation inhibitors were developed to target this issue (Heerboth et al., 2014).

The Mechanism Underlying Cardiovascular Diseases

Epigenetic therapy can be used for many disorders and diseases in various areas of the body, including the cardiovascular system, neurology, metabolic disorders, and cancer (Heerboth et al., 2014). It is important to have sufficient knowledge regarding the specific epigenetic changes that are associated with diseases that function on the development of specific inhibitors. This is due to the fact that this feature can be further devised into epigenetic drugs, which can be used in a variety of clinical settings to facilitate patient treatment (Heerboth et al., 2014). This section will cover the mechanistic bases for epigenetic therapy underlying cardiovascular diseases.

As an emerging area of research, cardiovascular diseases are responsible for nearly half of the non-communicable diseases that we see in our worldwide human population (Laslett et al., 2012). Globally, cardiovascular diseases account for approximately 17.3 million deaths per year, which has been hypothesized to grow to over 23.6 million by the year 2030 (Laslett et al., 2012). There has been an increasing amount of research on determining the correlation between histone and CpG residue modifications and how these factors are important for regulating cardiovascular functioning. However, the mechanistic process has not been fully elucidated and is currently not well understood (Heerboth et al., 2014). Angiogenesis is defined as the generation of new capillaries through the process of sprouting pre-existing microvessels (Rodríguez-Nieto et al., 2002). Vessel proliferation needs to be tightly regulated to prevent the onset of pathological diseases, including solid tumour progression, metastasis, diabetic retinopathy, hemangiomas, arthritis, psoriasis, and atherosclerosis (Rodríguez-Nieto et al., 2002). Angiogenesis suppression can be caused by elevated serum homocysteine levels and decreased nitric oxide production (Heerboth et al., 2014). There has been an increasing amount of epidemiological studies that show a strong association between high homocysteine levels and an increased risk of developing atherosclerotic cardiovascular disease (Mattson et al., 2002). Homocysteine is defined as a sulfur-containing, non-proteinogenic amino acid which takes a key place in between the folate cycle and the activated methyl cycle (Rodríguez-Nieto et al., 2002). Homocysteine modulates glutathione peroxidase expression, nitric oxide bioavailability, and endothelin-1 production (Rodríguez-Nieto et al., 2002). This is done through the production of reactive oxygen species and increasing the catalytic activity of copper ions in serum, which induces apoptosis (programmed cell death) in endothelial cells. Homocysteine increases the expression of endothelial cell surface adhesion molecules that are linked to vascular diseases, such as ICAM-1 and PAI-1. In the absence of oxidative stress, human endothelial cells can also undergo apoptosis due to increased homocysteine levels. The dysregulation of homocysteine, also known as hyperhomocysteinemia, leads to an increased risk of developing cardiovascular disease, which includes atherosclerosis (the development of plaque in arterial walls) and thrombosis (blood clotting). High levels of homocysteine induce pro-coagulant effects, which include the inhibition of protein-C activation, antithrombin III, and thrombomodulin (Rodríguez-Nieto et al., 2002).

During embryogenesis, the dysregulation of DNA methylation may lead to congenital heart disease and an increased risk of cardiovascular disease during adulthood. Researchers are currently investigating which genes are over-methylated, a condition which puts patients at an increased chance of developing cardiovascular disease (Heerboth et al., 2014). Epigenetic alterations have also been linked to upregulating the development of atherosclerosis and cardiovascular diseases. Researchers have found that atheroprotective estrogen receptor genes (known as ESR1 and ESR2) are often hypermethylated in patients with atherosclerosis. The mechanism explaining this process is linked to increasing age, as vascular damage is more likely to result for older patients. In normal and healthy individuals, the ESR genes are expressed at regular levels. However, the ESR gene levels decrease as a patient increases in age, which causes vascular damage (Heerboth et al., 2014).

Long-term, investigatory studies have provided early evidence that the fetal environment has large impacts on predicting the likelihood of developing chronic disorders going into adulthood. Epidemiological data shows that there are historical cohorts and demographic factors that predict an increased prevalence of cardiovascular disease, which leads to higher rates of infant mortality. Further analytical studies have shown that there is an inverse relationship between birth weight and susceptibility to cardiovascular morbidities, including hypertension, type 2 diabetes mellitus, hyperlipidemia, obesity, and insulin resistance. The hypothesis that explains these findings postulate that "fetal metabolic adjustments in nutritionally adverse circumstances that aim to restrict growth and thus safeguard brain development may result in an increased risk of chronic disorders in later stages of life" (Gluckman et al., 2009).

There are many epigenetic changes that are used to characterize metabolic diseases. As mentioned previously, epigenetic factors can play a repressive role in modulating gene function. Decreased histone H3 methylation is one of these repressive factors, which pairs with the increased expression of proinflammatory genes. These factors have been found to be involved in underlying the sustained proinflammatory phenotype of vascular smooth muscle cells. When vascular endothelial cells present features of histone H3 methylation, this signals for specific changes that result in the expression of proatherogenic genes. These genes are further linked to transient hyperglycemia, which is seen in diabetic animals - even after normalization of glycemia (Gluckman et al., 2009).

Nutritional research has shown that "folic acid deficiency also portrays an epigenetic link to endothelial dysfunction, which is related to several cardiovascular diseases" (Heerboth et al., 2014). Monitoring folic acid levels during pregnancy is a very important factor for expectant mothers to consider. Studies have shown that babies who were born to women that have a dietary deficiency in folic acid, also known as folate, are at an increased risk for moderate to severe birth defects that are targeted towards the nervous system. Insufficient amounts of folate can also lead to neural tube defects in the developing embryos of pregnant women, such as spina bifida, meningocele, encephalocele and anencephaly (Mattson et al., 2002). To help offset and prevent these defects from forming during pregnancy, mothers are advised to take dietary folate supplements. In adults, folate deficiencies present more susceptibility to developing several types of cardiovascular diseases, including coronary artery disease, stroke, cancer, Alzheimer's and Parkinson's disease. In addition, it was found that lower folate levels present an increased risk for colorectal cancer in young adults. Recent epidemiological evidence suggests that folate, calcium, and antioxidants are protective against cancer and/or polyps, whereas iron increases the risk of developing these health conditions (Tseng et al., 1996).

Generational Trauma

After a person experiences a traumatic event, they become susceptible to intergenerational trauma. This concept acknowledges the fact that exposure to extremely adverse events impacts individuals to such a great extent that their offspring find themselves grappling with their parents' post-traumatic state (Yehuda & Lehrner, 2018). In certain clinical scenarios, there may be an absence of biological explanations to explain observed or reported findings. In these cases, healthcare professionals resorted to using psychodynamic or behavioural perspectives to support the patient's overall health and well-being. For example, it has been suggested that "trauma survivors externalized their post-traumatic symptoms through their nonverbal behaviours and unconscious reenactments of fear and grief, such that the child became a container for the unwanted, troubling experiences of the parent" (Yehuda & Lehrner, 2018). To help mitigate the adverse effects associated with generational trauma, regular exercise and intensive learning have been suggested to help reverse epigenetic effects on the brain. Based on our current understanding of psychotherapy, mindfulness techniques and cognitive behavioural therapy (CBT) have been shown to build new neural pathways that can be used in the healing of trauma (Shadows of the Past, n.d.). In addition to this, it has been found that there are "sex-specific epigenetic effects following trauma exposure and parental developmental stage at the time of exposure, [which] explain different effects of maternal and paternal trauma" (Yehuda & Lehrner, 2018).

Further investigatory studies of generational trauma have shown that the HPA axis is vulnerable to environmental perturbations. During development, a young child is subject to early developmental programming through the biological and environmental factors that support their growth. The dysregulation of stress neurocircuitry is a fundamental feature of mood and anxiety disorders. A well-known example commonly dates back to Holocaust survivors and other individuals who were exposed to trauma during their lifetime. Low levels of cortisol and increased glucocorticoid receptor sensitivity in these individuals suggest that exposure to trauma can leave a long-lasting biological signature in stress biology. This is now regarded as a catalyst for longer-term adaptations when studying the effects of trauma in affected individuals (Yehuda & Lehrner, 2018). It was also found that "children of mothers exposed to childhood trauma, particularly emotional abuse, had higher sympathetic nervous system activation, which might be a marker for vulnerability to anxiety, compared to children of mothers with low emotional abuse, an effect that remained significant after accounting for maternal PTSD and depression, and for child trauma exposure" (Yehuda & Lehrner, 2018).

Conclusion and Future Directions

This chapter has described how epigenetic events are reversible in response to biological and environmental factors in an individual's life. Modifications to the epigenome can move forwards and backwards, as there are many types of alterations that can be induced upon the DNA sequence. Depending on the scenario, the modification can be removed completely or restored to its original functional state. An "epigenetic code" could dictate the expression of a particular set of genes, in essence serving as an "on/off" switch for many cellular events. The field of epigenetics is expanding, as researchers work together to develop the best sensitivity and specificity for having greater control over this epigenetic switch, to improve health outcomes and quality of life for patients in need of epigenetic therapeutic interventions.

References

Chapter 1

1. **Substance Abuse and Mental Health Services Administration. DSM-5 Changes: Implications for Child Serious Emotional Disturbance [Internet].** Rockville (MD): Substance Abuse and Mental Health Services Administration (US); 2016 Jun. Table 8, DSM-IV to DSM-5 Post-traumatic Stress Disorder Comparison Children 6 Years and Younger. Available from: https://www.ncbi.nlm.nih.gov/books/NBK519712/table/ch3.t4/
2. **Cloitre M, Garvert DW, Brewin CR, Bryant RA, Maercker A.** Evidence for proposed ICD-11 PTSD and complex PTSD: A latent profile analysis. Eur J Psychotraumatol. 2013;4. doi:10.3402/ejpt.v4i0.20706
3. **Life expectancy of First Nations, Métis and Inuit household populations in Canada. (2019, December 18).** Statistics Canada. https://www150.statcan.gc.ca/n1/pub/82-003-x/2019012/article/00001-eng.htm
4. **Bombay A, Matheson K, Anisman H.** The intergenerational effects of Indian Residential Schools: implications for the concept of historical trauma. Transcult Psychiatry. 2014 Jun;51(3):320-38. doi: 10.1177/1363461513503380. Epub 2013 Sep 24. PMID: 24065606; PMCID: PMC4232330.
5. **Dickson, C., & Watson, B. (2021, May 27).** Remains of 215 children found buried at former B.C. residential school, First Nation says. CBC. https://www.cbc.ca/news/canada/british-columbia/tk-eml%C3%BAps-te-

secw%C3%A9pemc-215-children-former-kamloops-indian-residential-school-1.6043778.
6. **Williams, M. T., Printz, D. M. B., & DeLapp, R. C. T. (2018).** Assessing racial trauma with the Trauma Symptoms of Discrimination Scale. Psychology of Violence, 8(6), 735–747. https://doi.org/10.1037/vio0000212

Chapter 2

1. **Neven, K. Y., Saenen, N. D., Tarantini, L., Janssen, B. G., Lefebvre, W., Vanpoucke, C., Bollati, V., & Nawrot, T. S. (2018).** Placental promoter methylation of DNA repair genes and prenatal exposure to particulate air pollution: an ENVIRONAGE cohort study. The Lancet. *Planetary health, 2*(4), e174–e183. https://doi.org/10.1016/S2542-5196(18)30049-4
2. **Rider CF., Carlsten C. (2019)** Air pollution and DNA methylation: effects of exposure in humans. *Clin Epigenet 11,* 131. https://doi.org/10.1186/s13148-019-0713-2
3. **Prunicki, M., Cauwenberghs, N., Lee, J., Zhou, X., Movassagh, H., Noth, E., Lurmann, F., Hammond, S. K., Balmes, J. R., Desai, M., Wu, J. C., & Nadeau, K. C. (2021).** Air pollution exposure is linked with methylation of immunoregulatory genes, altered immune cell profiles, and increased blood pressure in children. Scientific reports, 11(1), 4067. https://doi.org/10.1038/s41598-021-83577-3
4. **Felsenfeld G. (2014).** A brief history of epigenetics. *Cold Spring Harbor perspectives in biology, 6*(1), a018200. https://doi.org/10.1101/cshperspect.a018200
5. **Muller, H. J. (1930).** Types of visible variations induced by X-rays in Drosophila. *Journal of genetics, 22*(3), 299-

334.
6. **Valsiner J. (2007).** Gilbert Gottlieb's theory of probabilistic epigenesis: probabilities and realities in development. *Developmental psychobiology, 49*(8), 832–840. https://doi.org/10.1002/dev.20276
7. **Jarrell, D. K., Lennon, M. L., & Jacot, J. G. (2019).** Epigenetics and Mechanobiology in Heart Development and Congenital Heart Disease. *Diseases (Basel, Switzerland), 7*(3), 52. https://doi.org/10.3390/diseases7030052
8. **Boselli F, Steed E, Freund JB, Vermot J. (2017).** Anisotropic shear stress patterns predict the orientation of convergent tissue movements in the embryonic heart. *Development. 144,* 4322-4327; https://doi.org/10.1242/dev.152124
9. **Freund J. B., Goetz J. G, Hill KL, Vermot J. (2012).** Fluid flows and forces in development: functions, features and biophysical principles. *Development. 139,* 3063; https://doi.org/10.1242/dev.085902
10. **Johnson, P. A., & Johnson, J. C. (2020).** Shedding light on maternal sunlight exposure during pregnancy and considerations for public health policy. *Health Science Inquiry, 11*(1), 112-118. https://doi.org/10.29173/hsi298
11. **Staples, J., Ponsonby, A. L., & Lim, L. (2010).** Low maternal exposure to ultraviolet radiation in pregnancy, month of birth, and risk of multiple sclerosis in offspring: longitudinal analysis. *Bmj,* 340. https://doi.org/10.1136/bmj.c1640
12. **Við Streym, S., Rejnmark, L., Mosekilde, L., & Vestergaard, P. (2013).** No effect of season of birth on risk of type 1 diabetes, cancer, schizophrenia and ischemic heart disease, while some variations may be seen for pneumonia and multiple sclerosis. *Dermato-endocrinology,*

5(2), 309–316. https://doi.org/10.4161/derm.22779
13. Sayers, A., & Tobias, J. H. (2009). Estimated maternal ultraviolet B exposure levels in pregnancy influence skeletal development of the child. *The Journal of clinical endocrinology and metabolism, 94*(3), 765–771. https://doi.org/10.1210/jc.2008-2146
14. Tustin, K., Gross, J., & Hayne, H. (2004). Maternal exposure to first-trimester sunshine is associated with increased birth weight in human infants. *Developmental psychobiology, 45*(4), 221–230. https://doi.org/10.1002/dev.20030
15. Bianco-Miotto, T., Craig, J. M., Gasser, Y. P., van Dijk, S. J., & Ozanne, S. E. (2017). Epigenetics and DOHaD: from basics to birth and beyond. *Journal of developmental origins of health and disease, 8*(5), 513–519. https://doi.org/10.1017/S2040174417000733
16. Aboriginal Healing Foundation (AHF) (2003). Mental Health Profiles for a Sample of British Columbia's Aboriginal Survivors of the Canadian Residential School System. Ottawa: Aboriginal Healing Foundation. http://www.ahf.ca/downloads/mental-health.pdf
17. Mosby, I., & Galloway, T. (2017). "Hunger was never absent": How residential school diets shaped current patterns of diabetes among Indigenous peoples in Canada. *Cmaj, 189*(32), E1043-E1045. https://doi.org/10.1503/cmaj.170448

Chapter 3

Allarakha, S., & Suyog Uttekar, P. (2021, February 8). *What Are the 3 Types of Trauma?* MedicineNet. https://www.medicinenet.com/what_are_the_3_types_of_trauma/article.html

Bannister, A. J., & Kouzarides, T. (2011). Regulation of chromatin by histone modifications. *Cell Research, 21*(3), 381–395. https://doi.org/10.1038/cr.2011.22

Canadian Cancer Society. (n.d.). *Which cancers are hereditary?* - Canadian Cancer Society. Www.Cancer.Ca. Retrieved July 11, 2021, from https://www.cancer.ca:443/en/prevention-and-screening/reduce-cancer-risk/make-informed-decisions/check-family-history/which-cancers-are-hereditary/?region=bc

Eckhardt, F., Beck, S., Gut, I. G., & Berlin, K. (2004). Future potential of the Human Epigenome Project. Expert *Review of Molecular Diagnostics, 4*(5), 609–618. https://doi.org/10.1586/14737159.4.5.609

Kellermann, N. P. F. (2013). *Epigenetic Transmission of Holocaust Trauma: Can Nightmares Be Inherited?* 7.

Shadows of the Past: Epigenetics and Patterns of Inherited Trauma - iCAAD. (n.d.). Retrieved July 11, 2021, from https://www.icaad.com/blog/shadows-of-the-past-epigenetics-and-patterns-of-inherited-trauma

Skinner, M. K. (2014). Environmental stress and epigenetic transgenerational inheritance. *BMC Medicine, 12*(1), 153. https://doi.org/10.1186/s12916-014-0153-y

Stotz, K., & Griffiths, P. (2016). Epigenetics: Ambiguities and implications. *History and Philosophy of the Life Sciences, 38*(4), 22. https://doi.org/10.1007/s40656-016-0121-2

Tammen, S. A., Friso, S., & Choi, S.-W. (2013). Epigenetics: The link between nature and nurture. *Molecular Aspects of Medicine, 34*(4), 753–764. https://doi.org/10.1016/j.mam.2012.07.018

The Human Genome Project. (n.d.). Genome.Gov. Retrieved July 15, 2021, from https://www.genome.gov/human-genome-project

Witherington, D. C., & Lickliter, R. (2017). Transcending the Nature-Nurture Debate through Epigenetics: Are We There Yet? *Human Development, 60*(2/3), 65–68.

Chapter 4

Britannica, T. Editors of Encyclopaedia (2013, July 21). Histone. *Encyclopedia Britannica.* https://www.britannica.com/science/histone

Cooper, G. (2000). *The Cell: A Molecular Approach (2nd ed.).* Sinauer Associates Inc.

Cui, C., Shu, W., & Li, P. (2016). Fluorescence In situ Hybridization: Cell-Based Genetic Diagnostic and Research

Applications. *Frontiers in cell and developmental biology, 4,* 89. https://doi.org/10.3389/fcell.2016.00089

Das, P. M., Ramachandran, K., vanWert, J., & Singal, R. (2004). Chromatin immunoprecipitation assay. *BioTechniques, 37*(6), 961–969. https://doi.org/10.2144/04376rv01

Dostie J et al. (2006). Chromosome Conformation Capture Carbon Copy (5C): a massively parallel solution for mapping interactions between genomic elements. *Genome Res 10, 1299*–1309. PMID: 16954542

Ficz G et al. (2011). Dynamic regulation of 5-hydroxymethylcytosine in mouse ES cells and during differentiation. *Nature 473,* 398–402. PMID: 21460836

Gavrilov A et al. (2009). Chromosome conformation capture (from 3C to 5C) and its ChIP-based modification. *Methods Mol Biol 567, 171*–188. PMID: 19588093

Hagège, H. (2007, July 5). Quantitative analysis of chromosome... Nature Protocols. https://www.nature.com/articles/nprot.2007.243?error=cookies_not_supported&code=fb7f416e-e946-42df-9aec-43f456c855b5#Sec1

Hashimoto, K., Kokubun, S., Itoi, E., & Roach, H. I. (2007). Improved Quantification of DNA Methylation Using Methylation-Sensitive Restriction Enzymes and Real-Time PCR. *Epigenetics, 2*(2), 86–91. https://doi.org/10.4161/epi.2.2.4203

Li, Y., & Tollefsbol, T. O. (2011). DNA methylation detection: bisulfite genomic sequencing analysis. *Methods in molecular biology (Clifton, N.J.), 791*, 11–21. https://doi.org/10.1007/978-1-61779-316-5_2

Liu, L., Li, Y., & Tollefsbol, T. O. (2008). Gene-environment interactions and epigenetic basis of human diseases. Current issues in molecular biology, 10(1-2), 25–36.

Ohlsson R and Göndör A (2007). The 4C technique: the 'Rosetta stone' for genome biology in 3D? *Curr Opin Cell Biol 19, 321*–325. PMID: 17466501

Quantitative PCR: Things to Consider. (2017, January 1). ScienceDirect. https://www.sciencedirect.com/science/article/pii/B9780128026830000046

Song, L., & Crawford, G. E. (2010). DNase-seq: a high-resolution technique for mapping active gene regulatory elements across the genome from mammalian cells. Cold *Spring Harbor protocols, 2010*(2), pdb.prot5384. https://doi.org/10.1101/pdb.prot5384

Ruskin, H., & Barat, A. (2017). Recent advances in computational epigenetics. Advances in Genomics and Genetics, Volume 8, 1–12. https://doi.org/10.2147/agg.s115524

Srinivasan, M., Sedmak, D., & Jewell, S. (2002). Effect of fixatives and tissue processing on the content and integrity of nucleic acids. *The American journal of pathology, 161*(6), 1961–1971. https://doi.org/10.1016/S0002-9440(10)64472-0

Thu, K. L., Vucic, E. A., Kennett, J. Y., Heryet, C., Brown, C. J., Lam, W. L., & Wilson, I. M. (2009). Methylated DNA immunoprecipitation. *Journal of visualized experiments : JoVE, (23)*, 935. https://doi.org/10.3791/935

Tollefsbol, T. O. (2004). Methods of Epigenetic Analysis. *Epigenetics Protocols, 001*–008. https://doi.org/10.1385/1-59259-828-5:001

Weinhold B. (2006). Epigenetics: the science of change. *Environmental health perspectives, 114*(3), A160–A167. https://doi.org/10.1289/ehp.114-a160

Wu, F., Olson, B. G., & Yao, J. (2016). DamID-seq: Genome-wide Mapping of Protein-DNA Interactions by High Throughput Sequencing of Adenine-methylated DNA Fragments. *Journal of visualized experiments : JoVE,* (107), e53620. https://doi.org/10.3791/53620

Chapter 5

Barel, E.; Van IJzndoorn, M. H.; & Sagi-Schwartz, A. et. al. (2010) Surviving the Holocaust: A Meta-Analysis of the Long-Term Sequelae of a Genocide. *Psychological Bulletin, 136*(5), 677-798.

Bezo, B., & Maggi, S. (2015). Living in "survival mode:" Intergenerational transmission of trauma from the Holodomor genocide of 1932–1933 in Ukraine. *Social Science & Medicine, 134*, 87–94. https://doi.org/10.1016/j.socscimed.2015.04.009

Brown-Rice, K. (2013). Examining the Theory of Historical Trauma Among Native Americans. *The Professional Counselor, 3*(3), 117–130. https://doi.org/10.15241/kbr.3.3.117

Cassidy, J., Jones, J. D., & Shaver, P. R. (2013). Contributions of attachment theory and research: a framework for future research, translation, and policy. *Development and psychopathology, 25*(4 Pt 2), 1415–1434. https://doi.org/10.1017/S0954579413000692

DeAngelis, T. (2019, February). The legacy of trauma. *Monitor on Psychology, 50*(2). http://www.apa.org/monitor/2019/02/legacy-trauma

Doucet, M., & Rovers, M. (2010). Generational Trauma, Attachment, and Spiritual/Religious Interventions. *Journal of Loss and Trauma, 15*(2), 93–105. https://doi.org/10.1080/15325020903373078

Field, N. P.; Om, C.; & Kim, T. et. al. (2011) Parental styles in second generation effects of genocide stemming from the Khmer Rouge regime in Cambodia. *Attachment and human development, 13*(6), 611-628.

Fossion, P., Rejas, M. C., Servais, L., Pelc, I., & Hirsch, S. (2003). Family Approach with Grandchildren of Holocaust Survivors. *American Journal of Psychotherapy, 57*(4), 519–527. https://doi.org/10.1176/appi.psychotherapy.2003.57.4.519

Gillespie, C. (2020, December 9). *What Is Generational Trauma? Here's How Experts Explain It.* Health.Com. https://www.health.com/condition/ptsd/generational-trauma

Motta, R. W., Joseph, J. M., Rose, R. D., Suozzi, J. M., & Leiderman, L. J. (1997). Secondary trauma: Assessing inter-generational transmission of war experiences with a modified Stroop procedure. *Journal of Clinical Psychology, 53*(8), 895–903. https://doi.org/10.1002/(SICI)1097-4679(199712)53:8%3C895::AID-JCLP14%3E3.0.CO;2-F

Pisano, N. G. (2012) Chapter 2: Research Approach. Granddaughters of the Holocaust: Never Forgetting What They Didn't Experience. (pp. 47-50) Academic Studies Press.

Shapiro, J., Douglas, K., de la Rocha, O., Radecki, S., Vu, C., & Dinh, T. (1999). Generational Differences in Psychosocial Adaptation and Predictors of Psychological Distress in a Population of Recent Vietnamese Immigrants. *Journal of Community Health, 24*(2), 95–113. https://doi.org/10.1023/a:1018702323648

Sigal, J. J., & Rakoff, V. (1971). Concentration Camp Survival: A Pilot Study of Effects on the Second Generation. *Canadian Psychiatric Association Journal, 16*(5), 393–397. https://doi.org/10.1177/070674377101600503

West, S. K. & Hollis, M. (2012) Barriers to Completion of Advance Care Directives among African Americans Ages 25-84: A Cross-Generational Study. Omega (Westport), 65(2), 125-137.

Chapter 6

Bokar, J. A. (2005). The biosynthesis and functional roles of methylated nucleosides in eukaryotic mRNA. In H. Grosjean (Ed.), Fine-Tuning of RNA Functions by Modification and Editing (pp. 141–177). Springer. https://doi.org/10.1007/b106365

Brennecke, J., Stark, A., Russell, R. B., & Cohen, S. M. (2005). Principles of MicroRNA–Target Recognition. *PLoS Biology, 3*(3), e85. https://doi.org/10.1371/journal.pbio.0030085

Centers for Disease Control and Prevention. (2018, October 9). *Prion Diseases | CDC.* https://www.cdc.gov/prions/index.html

Garber, K. (2019, July 1). Hidden layer of gene control influences everything from cancer to memory. Science | AAAS. https://www.sciencemag.org/news/2019/07/hidden-layer-gene-control-influences-everything-cancer-memory

Gibney, E. R., & Nolan, C. M. (2010). Epigenetics and gene expression. *Heredity, 105*(1), 4–13. https://doi.org/10.1038/hdy.2010.54

Harvey, Z. H., Chen, Y., & Jarosz, D. F. (2018). Protein-Based Inheritance: Epigenetics beyond the Chromosome. *Molecular Cell, 69*(2), 195–202. https://doi.org/10.1016/j.molcel.2017.10.030

Jia, G., Fu, Y., Zhao, X., Dai, Q., Zheng, G., Yang, Y., Yi, C., Lindahl, T., Pan, T., Yang, Y.-G., & He, C. (2011). N6-Methyladenosine in Nuclear RNA is a Major Substrate of the Obesity-Associated FTO. *Nature Chemical Biology, 7*(12), 885–887. https://doi.org/10.1038/nchembio.687

Karikó, K., Buckstein, M., Ni, H., & Weissman, D. (2005). Suppression of RNA Recognition by Toll-like Receptors: The Impact of Nucleoside Modification and the Evolutionary Origin of RNA. *Immunity, 23*(2), 165–175. https://doi.org/10.1016/j.immuni.2005.06.008

Khalil, A. M., Guttman, M., Huarte, M., Garber, M., Raj, A., Rivea Morales, D., Thomas, K., Presser, A., Bernstein, B. E., van Oudenaarden, A., Regev, A., Lander, E. S., & Rinn, J. L. (2009). Many human large intergenic noncoding RNAs associate with chromatin-modifying complexes and affect gene expression. *Proceedings of the National Academy of Sciences of the United States of America, 106*(28), 11667–11672. https://doi.org/10.1073/pnas.0904715106

Lim, L. P., Lau, N. C., Garrett-Engele, P., Grimson, A., Schelter, J. M., Castle, J., Bartel, D. P., Linsley, P. S., & Johnson, J. M. (2005). Microarray analysis shows that some microRNAs downregulate large numbers of target mRNAs. *Nature, 433*(7027), 769–773. https://doi.org/10.1038/nature03315

Liu, B., Larsson, L., Caballero, A., Hao, X., Öling, D., Grantham, J., & Nyström, T. (2010). The Polarisome Is Required for Segregation and Retrograde Transport of Protein Aggregates. *Cell, 140*(2), 257–267. https://doi.org/10.1016/j.cell.2009.12.031

Liu, N., & Pan, T. (2015). RNA epigenetics. Translational Research : *The Journal of Laboratory and Clinical Medicine*, *165*(1), 28–35. https://doi.org/10.1016/j.trsl.2014.04.003

Manjrekar, J. (2017). Epigenetic inheritance, prions and evolution. *Journal of Genetics, 96*(3), 445–456. https://doi.org/10.1007/s12041-017-0798-3

Pardi, N., Hogan, M. J., Porter, F. W., & Weissman, D. (2018). mRNA vaccines—A new era in vaccinology. Nature Reviews *Drug Discovery, 17*(4), 261–279. https://doi.org/10.1038/nrd.2017.243

Rinn, J. L., Kertesz, M., Wang, J. K., Squazzo, S. L., Xu, X., Brugmann, S. A., Goodnough, H., Helms, J. A., Farnham, P. J., Segal, E., & Chang, H. Y. (2007). Functional Demarcation of Active and Silent Chromatin Domains in Human HOX Loci by Non-Coding RNAs. *Cell, 129*(7), 1311–1323. https://doi.org/10.1016/j.cell.2007.05.022

Sætrom, P., Snøve, O., & Rossi, J. J. (2007). Epigenetics and MicroRNAs. *Pediatric Research, 61*(7), 17–23. https://doi.org/10.1203/pdr.0b013e318045760e

Shah, P. K., Narendran, V., & Kalpana, N. (2009). Aicardi syndrome: The importance of an ophthalmologist in its diagnosis. *Indian Journal of Ophthalmology, 57*(3), 234–236. https://doi.org/10.4103/0301-4738.49403

Simmons, D. (2008). Epigenetic Influences and Disease. *Scitable by Nature Education.* http://www.nature.com/scitable/topicpage/epigenetic-influences-and-disease-895

Smalheiser, N. R., & Torvik, V. I. (2005). Mammalian microRNAs derived from genomic repeats. *Trends in Genetics, 21*(6), 322–326. https://doi.org/10.1016/j.tig.2005.04.008

Statello, L., Guo, C.-J., Chen, L.-L., & Huarte, M. (2021). Gene regulation by long non-coding RNAs and its biological functions. *Nature Reviews Molecular Cell Biology, 22*(2), 96–118. https://doi.org/10.1038/s41580-020-00315-9

Tian, S., Lai, J., Yu, T., Li, Q., & Chen, Q. (2021). Regulation of Gene Expression Associated With the N6-Methyladenosine (m6A) Enzyme System and Its Significance in Cancer. *Frontiers in Oncology, 0*. https://doi.org/10.3389/fonc.2020.623634

Wilusz, J. E., Sunwoo, H., & Spector, D. L. (2009). Long noncoding RNAs: Functional surprises from the RNA world. *Genes & Development, 23*(13), 1494–1504. https://doi.org/10.1101/gad.1800909

Zhou, C., Slaughter, B. D., Unruh, J. R., Guo, F., Yu, Z., Mickey, K., Narkar, A., Ross, R. T., McClain, M., & Li, R. (2014). Organelle-Based Aggregation and Retention of Damaged Proteins in Asymmetrically Dividing Cells. *Cell, 159*(3), 530–542. https://doi.org/10.1016/j.cell.2014.09.026

Chapter 7

Porter, A. N. (2016). *European Imperialism, 1860-1914.*

Taylor, C. C. (2020). *Sacrifice as terror: The Rwandan genocide of 1994.* Routledge.

Shohat, E., & Stam, R. (2014). *Unthinking Eurocentrism: Multiculturalism and the media.* Routledge.

Farmer, P. (2004). An anthropology of structural violence. *Current anthropology, 45*(3), 305-325.

Muñoz, J. E. G., Rodriguez, A., Raso, J. E. G., & Cuesta, J. A. (2009). Genetic evidence for cryptic speciation in the freshwater shrimp genus Atyaephyra de Brito Capello (Crustacea, Decapoda, Atyidae). *Zootaxa, 2025*(1), 32-42.

Gaddis, J. L. (2006). *The Cold War: a new history.* Penguin.

Whitfield, S. J. (1996). *The culture of the Cold War.* JHU Press.

Major, P. (2010). *Behind the Berlin Wall: East Germany and the frontiers of power.* Oxford University Press.

Gareis, S. B. (2012). *The United Nations.* Macmillan International Higher Education.

Gordon, T. (2006). *Canada, empire and indigenous people in the Americas.* Socialist Studies/Études Socialistes.

Francis, M. (1998). *The" civilizing" of indigenous people in nineteenth-century Canada.* Journal of World History, 51-87.

Grant, A. (1996). *No End of Grief: Indian Residential Schools in Canada.* Pemmican Publications, Inc., 1635 Burrows Ave., Winnipeg, Manitoba, Canada R2X 0T1.

Lavallee, L. F., & Poole, J. M. (2010). Beyond recovery: Colonization, health and healing for Indigenous people in Canada. *International journal of mental health and addiction, 8*(2), 271-281.

Allières, J. (2016). *The Basques.*

Aguirre, A., Vicario, A., Mazón, L. I., Estomba, A., de Pancorbo, M. M., Picó, V. A., ... & Lostao, C. M. (1991). Are the Basques a single and a unique population?. *American journal of human genetics, 49*(2), 450.

Molina, F. (2010). The historical dynamics of ethnic conflicts: confrontational nationalisms, democracy and the Basques in contemporary Spain. *Nations and Nationalism, 16*(2), 240-260.

Chapter 8

Bajrami, E., & Spiroski, M. (2016). Genomic Imprinting. *Open access Macedonian journal of medical sciences, 4*(1), 181–184. https://doi.org/10.3889/oamjms.2016.028

Centers for Disease Control and Prevention. (2020, August 3). *What is Epigenetics?* Centers for Disease Control and Prevention. https://www.cdc.gov/genomics/disease/epigenetics.htm#:~:text=Epigenetics%20is%20the%20study%20of,body%20reads%20a%20DNA%20sequence.

Cheng, Y., He, C., Wang, M., Ma, X., Mo, F., Yang, S., Han, J., & Wei, X. (2019). Targeting epigenetic regulators for cancer therapy: mechanisms and advances in clinical trials. *Signal Transduction and Targeted Therapy, 4*(1). https://doi.org/10.1038/s41392-019-0095-0

Lobo, I. (2008). *Genomic Imprinting and Patterns of Disease Inheritance.* Nature News. https://www.nature.com/scitable/topicpage/genomic-imprinting-and-patterns-of-disease-inheritance-899/.

Mayo Foundation for Medical Education and Research. (2020, February 4). *Angelman syndrome.* Mayo Clinic. https://www.mayoclinic.org/diseases-conditions/angelman-syndrome/symptoms-causes/syc-20355621.

Mayo Foundation for Medical Education and Research. (2020, October 30). *Diabetes.* Mayo Clinic. https://www.mayoclinic.org/diseases-conditions/diabetes/symptoms-causes/syc-20371444.

Melén, E., Barouki, R., Barry, M., Boezen, H. M., Hoffmann, B., Krauss-Etschmann, S., Koppelman, G. H., & Forsberg, B. (2018, April 1). *Promoting respiratory public health through epigenetics research: an ERS Environment Health Committee workshop report.* European Respiratory Society. https://erj.ersjournals.com/content/51/4/1702410.

Murri, M., Leiva, I., Gomez-Zumaquero, J. M., Tinahones, F. J., Cardona, F., Soriguer, F., et al. (2013). *Gut microbiota in children with type 1 diabetes differs from that in healthy children: a case-control study.* BMC Med. 11, 46. doi: 10.1186/1741-7015-11-46.

National Institute on Drug Abuse. (2019, August 5). *Genetics and Epigenetics of Addiction DrugFacts.* Retrieved from https://www.drugabuse.gov/publications/drugfacts/genetics-epigenetics-addiction on 2021, July 15

Sharma, M., Li, Y., Stoll, M. L., & Tollefsbol, T. O. (2020). *The Epigenetic Connection Between the Gut Microbiome in Obesity and Diabetes.* Frontiers in Genetics, 10. https://doi.org/10.3389/fgene.2019.01329

The Public Engagement team at the Wellcome Genome Campus. (2016, January 25). *What are dominant and recessive alleles?* Facts. https://www.yourgenome.org/facts/what-are-dominant-and-recessive-alleles.

Tyler, M. (2018, May 25). *What Is Addiction?* Healthline. https://www.healthline.com/health/addiction#treatment.

U.S. National Library of Medicine. (2021, June 11). *What is epigenetics?:* . MedlinePlus. https://medlineplus.gov/genetics/understanding/howgeneswork/epigenome/.

U.S. National Library of Medicine. (2020, September 8). *Prader-Willi syndrome: MedlinePlus Genetics.* MedlinePlus. https://medlineplus.gov/genetics/condition/prader-willi-syndrome/#causes.

What Is Cancer? American Cancer Society. (2020). https://www.cancer.org/cancer/cancer-basics/what-is-cancer.html.

What Is Cancer? National Cancer Institute. (2021). https://www.cancer.gov/about-cancer/understanding/what-is-cancer.

World Health Organization. (2021, March 3). *Cancer.* World Health Organization. https://www.who.int/news-room/fact-sheets/detail/cancer.

Chapter 9

Cai, N., Fňašková, M., Konečná, K., Fojtová, M., Fajkus, J., Coomber, E., Watt, S., Soranzo, N., Preiss, M., & Rektor, I. (2020). No Evidence of Persistence or Inheritance of Mitochondrial DNA Copy Number in Holocaust Survivors and Their Descendants. *Frontiers in Genetics,* 0. https://doi.org/10.3389/fgene.2020.00087

Cai, N., Li, Y., Chang, S., Liang, J., Lin, C., Zhang, X., Liang, L., Hu, J., Chan, W., Kendler, K. S., Malinauskas, T., Huang, G.-J., Li, Q., Mott, R., & Flint, J. (2015). Genetic Control over mtDNA and Its Relationship to Major Depressive Disorder. *Current Biology, 25*(24), 3170–3177. https://doi.org/10.1016/j.cub.2015.10.065

Carey, B. (2018, December 10). *Can We Really Inherit Trauma?* The New York Times. https://www.nytimes.com/2018/12/10/health/mind-epigenetics-genes.html

Chen, Q., Yan, W., & Duan, E. (2016). Epigenetic inheritance of acquired traits through sperm RNAs and sperm RNA modifications. *Nature Reviews Genetics, 17*(12), 733–743. https://doi.org/10.1038/nrg.2016.106

Danchin, É., Charmantier, A., Champagne, F. A., Mesoudi, A., Pujol, B., & Blanchet, S. (2011). Beyond DNA: Integrating inclusive inheritance into an extended theory of evolution. *Nature Reviews Genetics, 12*(7), 475–486. https://doi.org/10.1038/nrg3028

Gillespie, C. (2020, October 27). *Generational Trauma Might Explain Your Anxiety and Depression-Here's What It Means.* Health.Com. https://www.health.com/condition/ptsd/generational-trauma

Horsthemke, B. (2018). A critical view on transgenerational epigenetic inheritance in humans. *Nature Communications, 9*(1), 2973. https://doi.org/10.1038/s41467-018-05445-5

Mulligan, C., D'Errico, N., Stees, J., & Hughes, D. (2012). Methylation changes at NR3C1 in newborns associate with maternal prenatal stress exposure and newborn birth weight. *Epigenetics, 7*(8), 853–857. https://doi.org/10.4161/epi.21180

Perroud, N., Rutembesa, E., Paoloni-Giacobino, A., Mutabaruka, J., Mutesa, L., Stenz, L., Malafosse, A., & Karege, F. (2014). The Tutsi genocide and transgenerational transmission of maternal stress: Epigenetics and biology of the HPA axis. *The World Journal of Biological Psychiatry, 15*(4), 334–345. https://doi.org/10.3109/15622975.2013.866693

Radtke, K. M., Ruf, M., Gunter, H. M., Dohrmann, K., Schauer, M., Meyer, A., & Elbert, T. (2011). Transgenerational impact of intimate partner violence on methylation in the promoter of the glucocorticoid receptor. *Translational Psychiatry, 1*(7), e21. https://doi.org/10.1038/tp.2011.21

Rodgers, A. B., Morgan, C. P., Bronson, S. L., Revello, S., & Bale, T. L. (2013). Paternal Stress Exposure Alters Sperm MicroRNA Content and Reprograms Offspring HPA Stress Axis Regulation. *The Journal of Neuroscience, 33*(21), 9003–9012. https://doi.org/10.1523/JNEUROSCI.0914-13.2013

Sharma, U., Sun, F., Conine, C. C., Reichholf, B., Kukreja, S., Herzog, V. A., Ameres, S. L., & Rando, O. J. (2018). Small RNAs are trafficked from the epididymis to developing mammalian sperm. *Developmental Cell, 46*(4), 481-494.e6. https://doi.org/10.1016/j.devcel.2018.06.023

Wylie, C., & Anderson, R. (2002). 9—Germ Cells. In J. Rossant & P. P. L. Tam (Eds.), Mouse Development (pp. 181–190). *Academic Press.* https://doi.org/10.1016/B978-012597951-1/50012-3

Yehuda, R., Daskalakis, N. P., Bierer, L. M., Bader, H. N., Klengel, T., Holsboer, F., & Binder, E. B. (2016). Holocaust Exposure Induced Intergenerational Effects on FKBP5 Methylation. *Biological Psychiatry, 80*(5), 372–380. https://doi.org/10.1016/j.biopsych.2015.08.005

Yehuda, R., & Lehrner, A. (2018). Intergenerational transmission of trauma effects: Putative role of epigenetic mechanisms. *World Psychiatry, 17*(3), 243–257. https://doi.org/10.1002/wps.20568

Youssef, N. A., Lockwood, L., Su, S., Hao, G., & Rutten, B. P. F. (2018). The Effects of Trauma, with or without PTSD, on the Transgenerational DNA Methylation Alterations in Human Offsprings. *Brain Sciences, 8*(5), 83. https://doi.org/10.3390/brainsci8050083

Chapter 10

Gluckman, P. D., Hanson, M. A., Buklijas, T., Low, F. M., & Beedle, A. S. (2009). Epigenetic mechanisms that underpin metabolic and cardiovascular diseases. *Nature Reviews Endocrinology, 5*(7), 401–408. https://doi.org/10.1038/nrendo.2009.102

Heerboth, S., Lapinska, K., Snyder, N., Leary, M., Rollinson, S., & Sarkar, S. (2014). Use of Epigenetic Drugs in Disease: An Overview. *Genetics & Epigenetics, 6*, 9–19. https://doi.org/10.4137/GEG.S12270

Laslett, L. J., Alagona, P., Clark, B. A., Drozda, J. P., Saldivar, F., Wilson, S. R., Poe, C., & Hart, M. (2012). The Worldwide Environment of Cardiovascular Disease: Prevalence, Diagnosis, Therapy, and Policy Issues. *Journal of the American College of Cardiology, 60*(25_Supplement), S1–S49. https://doi.org/10.1016/j.jacc.2012.11.002

Mattson, M. P., Kruman, I. I., & Duan, W. (2002). Folic acid and homocysteine in age-related disease. *Ageing Research Reviews, 1*(1), 95–111. https://doi.org/10.1016/S0047-6374(01)00365-7

Moore, L. D., Le, T., & Fan, G. (2013). DNA Methylation and Its Basic Function. *Neuropsychopharmacology, 38*(1), 23–38. https://doi.org/10.1038/npp.2012.112

Rodríguez-Nieto, S., Chavarría, T., Martínez-Poveda, B., Sánchez-Jiménez, F., Rodríguez Quesada, A., & Medina, M. Á. (2002). Anti-angiogenic effects of homocysteine on cultured endothelial cells. *Biochemical and Biophysical Research Communications, 293*(1), 497–500. https://doi.org/10.1016/S0006-291X(02)00232-2

Shadows of the Past: Epigenetics and Patterns of Inherited Trauma - iCAAD. (n.d.). Retrieved July 11, 2021, from https://www.icaad.com/blog/shadows-of-the-past-epigenetics-and-patterns-of-inherited-trauma

Tseng, M., Murray, S. C., Kupper, L. L., & Sandier, R. S. (1996). Micronutrients and the Risk of Colorectal Adenomas. *American Journal of Epidemiology, 144*(11), 1005–1014. https://doi.org/10.1093/oxfordjournals.aje.a008871

Yehuda, R., & Lehrner, A. (2018). Intergenerational transmission of trauma effects: Putative role of epigenetic mechanisms. *World Psychiatry, 17*(3), 243–257. https://doi.org/10.1002/wps.20568

www.ingramcontent.com/pod-product-compliance
Lightning Source LLC
Chambersburg PA
CBHW050113170426
43198CB00014B/2558